Marilyn G. Stewart
Sydney R. Walker

Rethinking Curriculum in Art

Davis Publications, Inc., Worcester, Massachusetts

ART EDUCATION IN PRACTICE SERIES

Marilyn G. Stewart

Editor

Marilyn G. Stewart and Sydney R. Walker

Rethinking Curriculum in Art

Series Preface

Follow an art teacher around for a day—and then stand amazed. At any given moment, the art teacher has a ready knowledge of materials available for making and responding to art; lesson plans with objectives for student learning; resources for extending art learning to other subjects; and the capabilities, interests, and needs of the students in the art room. Often working with a schedule that requires shifting several times a day from working with students in preschool to those in elementary, middle, and high school, the art teacher decides what to teach, how to teach it, whether students have learned it, and what to do next. The need for rapid decision making in the art room is relentless.

The demands continue after school as the art teacher engages in assessment of student learning, curriculum planning, organization of materials, and a wide range of activities within the school community. Although most teachers want to be aware of and to integrate into their teaching new findings and developments within their field, they are pressed to find the time for routine, extensive reading of the literature.

Art Education in Practice provides the art teacher, museum educator, student, scholar, and layperson involved in art education with an overview of significant topics in art education theory and practice. The series is designed to meet the needs of art educators who want to know the issues within, the rationales provided for, and the practical implications of accepting curricular proposals presented from a variety of scholarly and political perspectives.

The emphasis of the series is on informed practice. Each text focuses on a topic that has received considerable attention in art education literature and advocacy statements, but one that has not always been accompanied by clear, concise, and accessible recommendations for the classroom. As new issues arise, books will be added to the series. The goal of the series is to complement the professional libraries of practitioners in the field of art education and, in turn, enhance the art-related lives of their students.

Editor's Introduction

The rethinking of curriculum that this book puts forward was prompted by teacher engagement in a national effort to transform education through the arts. As described in Chapter 1 of this book, the Transforming Education Through the Arts Challenge, or TETAC project, was initiated by the National Arts Education Consortium, comprising six regional organizations in six states. A curriculum task force—Jean Detlefsen of Nebraska, Ann Rowson Love of Tennessee, Sydney Walker of Ohio, Nancy Walkup of Texas, Marilyn Wulliger of California, Ron Yrabedra of Florida, and I, who served as an evaluation consultant to the project—met several times during a period covering two years to create curriculum guidelines to assist teachers in developing or adapting curricula in the arts that linked to other core subjects.

These meetings were arranged by Donald Killeen, TETAC national program manager, and often included Joy Frechtling and Barbara Kapinus from the staff of Westat, the research firm involved with evaluation of the project. Because the TETAC representatives from the regional organizations also served as mentors to teachers in participating schools, they brought to the table the concerns and issues of the teachers with whom they worked. This input was crucial, as were findings from the project evaluators, current research, and school reform efforts, as we sought to guide the TETAC teachers in developing substantive, comprehensive arts-based curricula in their schools.

The task force developed curriculum guidelines categorized into five general sections: Unit Foundations, Content, Instruction, Assessment, and Design. Probably the most important addition to the more typical considerations in curriculum design was the emphasis on what we called the "enduring ideas" that have drawn the attention of humans though the ages and serve as the focus around which inquiry in the arts and other disciplines can be meaningfully integrated.

As the TETAC teachers in pre-K through 12 designed and implemented units of instruction, they learned to identify such enduring ideas and sets of related key concepts and essential questions. They created instructional strategies that embraced constructivist and inquiry-based practices, adjusted these to the diverse learning styles of students, and employed assessment strategies aimed toward identifying degrees of understanding on the part of their students. They routinely submitted their units for evaluation and feedback and worked to refine them based upon this feedback and their own careful reflection. Many of these TETAC teachers spoke of how the approach outlined in the curriculum guidelines changed forever the way they thought about teaching and learning. They truly came to rethink curriculum through the TETAC project.

When the steering committee of the National Arts Education Consortium deemed the *Art Education in Practice* series an appropriate venue for disseminating the findings of the TETAC project, Sydney Walker and I agreed to coauthor this text, which I am extremely proud to offer to the field. I am also humbled to know that the ideas and strategies suggested here represent the intense effort, dedication, and commitment of hundreds of educators across the nation who have worked and continue to work toward the recognition of the arts as rich and generative areas of study, in and of themselves, and as catalysts for substantive teaching and learning in today's schools.

Marilyn G. Stewart

Publisher: Wyatt Wade
Managing Editor: David Coen
Manufacturing: Georgiana Rock
Design: Jeannet Leendertse

Library of Congress Control Number: 2005929172

ISBN 0-87192-692-X
10 9 8 7 6 5 4 3 2 1
Printed in the United States of America

Contents

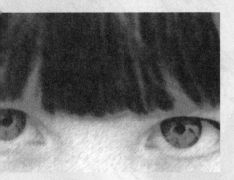

Chapter *5*

Chapter 6

Chapter 7

Chapter *8*

Acknowledgments

This book grew out of the work of the many participants—mentors, teachers, administrators, steering committee members, evaluators, and funders—involved with the five-year Transforming Education Through the Arts Challenge (TETAC) project. Our first debt of thanks belongs to the TETAC mentors from the six regional centers in California, Florida, Nebraska, Ohio, Tennessee, and Texas who tirelessly advised and consulted with the dedicated art and classroom teachers who participated in the project. Along with the TETAC mentors, we acknowledge the many teachers and their contributions to our understanding as the curriculum ideas became actualized in their classrooms; additionally, our colleagues on the Curriculum Task Force for the TETAC project, for nurturing the ideas that informed, shaped, and drove the project forward toward new ways of thinking about curriculum design and classroom practice; the TETAC National Steering Committee members and the TETAC national program manager, Don Killeen, for guiding the project as it evolved; and The J. Paul Getty Trust and The Annenberg Foundation, major funders of the TETAC project, for their support. Finally, we wish to thank our publisher, Wyatt Wade, our editor, David Coen, and the staff at Davis Publications for their fine work in shepherding this book to publication.

The TETAC Curriculum Task Force Members

Jean Detlefsen
Prairie Visions: Nebraska Consortium for Arts Education at the Nebraska Arts Council, Omaha, Nebraska

Ann Rowson Love
Southeast Center for Education in the Arts at the University of Tennessee, Chattanooga

Marilyn Stewart
Content Consultant to the Project, Kutztown University, Kutztown, Pennsylvania

Sydney Walker
Ohio Partnership for the Visual Arts at The Ohio State University, Columbus, Ohio

Nancy Walkup
North Texas Institute for Educators on the Visual Arts at the University of North Texas, Denton

Ron Yrabedra
Florida Institute for Arts Education at Florida State University, Tallahassee

Marilyn Wulliger
California Regional Consortium for Arts Education at the Sacramento County Office of Education, Sacramento, California

Chapter

1

Introduction

"Thinking deeply about what we are doing leads us to ask better questions, break out of fruitless routines, make unexpected connections and experiment with fresh ideas."
　—Ron Brandt

Ask art teachers if they ever think about their curricula and you will most likely find that they all do. Daily. Curriculum is necessarily dynamic. Curriculum documents tend to be static, but our day-to-day course of action shifts dynamically as we make choices about content, instruction, and assessment and as we reflect upon what seems to be working with our students and what needs to be rethought. Such choices reflect basic assumptions about what counts as important content in art, what kinds of instructional strategies are most effective, and how we can best assess how our students are achieving. We draw upon these deeply embedded notions as we make shifts in our plans and, in the process, the curriculum changes. In this sense, most teachers consistently rethink curriculum in art.

The focus of this book, however is not the planning shifts often required in teaching a given course but, rather, the deeply embedded assumptions that stand at the heart of general curriculum decision making. Our hope is that as art educators read this book, they will seriously examine their basic, foundational ideas about what is important for students to learn and how this learning can best be accomplished. The ideas put forward are in response to more than a decade of school reform efforts in education regarding teaching for understanding, accountability, student relevance, and the information and visual explosion stemming from the continued growth of media and technology. We believe that the research, theory, and new practice around these developments warrant a careful examination by those who care about the art education of today's children and youth. We also believe that today's teachers can benefit from assistance in their efforts—collaborative or alone—to construct or revise their art programs and curricula. The approaches outlined in this book represent the authors' attempt to address this need.

What's the "Big Idea"?

In our attempt to highlight connections between recent developments in educational theory, research, and new practice with art education content and purposes, we introduce the reader to a process for creating curricula in art. We show how the use of enduring ideas can serve as a foundation for art curricula and how the study of art can be linked, in substantive ways, to other subjects in general education. We focus on ways that enduring ideas can guide curriculum writers in meeting local, state, and national standards in art and, when appropriate, other relevant subject areas. We offer guidelines for selecting content, designing instruction, and creating various forms of assessment. Throughout the book, the reader will encounter numerous examples from actual units of study designed by teachers involved in a project entitled "Transforming Education Through the Arts Challenge" (TETAC), a five-year project completed in 2001 and funded, in part, by The Annenberg Foundation and the J. Paul Getty Trust.* Consistent with the approaches used in other books in the Art Education in Practice series, we include theoretical foundations, but primarily focus upon ways in which theory informs practice. Parts of the book guide the reader through step-by-step processes to follow in designing curriculum.

The work of the TETAC project was influenced by and built upon a decade of theory and practice in art education that focused on discipline-based art education (DBAE). In addition, the increasing attention in general education to interdisciplinary teaching and learning and other ideas consistent with recent school reform efforts influenced the project. The project included six major sites, each of which had served as a Getty Regional Institute during the decade of funding by the Getty Education Institute for the Arts. The six sites, located in California, Florida, Nebraska, Ohio, Tennessee, and Texas, formed the National Arts Education Consortium. As part of the TETAC project, each site selected five or six partner schools—including elementary, middle, and high schools—to serve as demonstration sites for implementing a comprehensive approach to arts education linked to whole school reform strategies to improve student achievement.

* Starting in the fall of 1996, the National Arts Education Consortium embarked on a five-year national educational reform initiative, the Transforming Education Through the Arts Challenge, to link comprehensive arts education with national and local efforts to reform our nation's schools. Information about this project can be found in the National Arts Education Consortium, Transforming Education Through the Arts Challenge: Final Project Report (Columbus, OH: Department of Art Education, Ohio State University), and at The Annenberg Challenge Archive Site (http://www.annenberginstitute.org/Challenge/sites/tetac.html).

Teachers in these partner schools worked with site mentors on a regular basis, providing feedback and designing units of instruction. Each school submitted two such units per year for evaluation and feedback.

The TETAC Curriculum Guidelines Committee, consisting of one representative from each of the six regional sites and a content consultant to the TETAC project, designed curriculum guidelines that provided the basis for curriculum design within the project. These guidelines also have provided the foundation for this book, along with examples from units of study submitted by teams of teachers in TETAC schools over the years. Although this book describes, and thus reports to the field, the important curriculum work of the TETAC project, it is primarily intended as a practical guide to developing curriculum for a comprehensive approach to the study of art within the framework of whole school reform.

1.1 Teachers in the TETAC project worked together to plan units of study and strategies to help their students respond to artworks.

Who Should Read This Book?

The primary audience for this book is in-service, or practicing, teachers and pre-service teachers—individuals studying in teacher preparation programs. Because of its relevance to interdisciplinary teaching and learning, it will also be useful for non–art teachers interested in ways to include the visual arts in substantive interdisciplinary curricula. In addition, we hope that the book will be useful for arts curriculum supervisors, museum educators, and arts administrators.

For pre-service art teachers, the contents of this book will introduce important concepts in curriculum design. Pre-service teachers can use these concepts to inform the curricula they plan as part of their study and training.

As teachers who are experienced in developing curricula for their own programs encounter the approaches outlined in this book, we hope they will

reconsider what they routinely do as they plan. The introduction of curriculum foundations, for example, with its emphasis on identifying enduring ideas, key concepts, and essential questions upon which units of study, lessons, activities, and assessment can be based, requires that even experienced teachers reflect more carefully upon why they do what they do in their own classrooms.

The so-called standards movement has resulted in increasing instances in which teachers are asked to create district-wide documents to address local, state, and/or national standards. To align curricula with standards and to provide broad frameworks for local curriculum development, school districts routinely engage groups of teachers in curriculum writing projects. For most teachers, this task is daunting. While art teachers often are very clear about what they do with their own students and how they plan individual lessons to address standards, they often

1.2 *In a comprehensive approach to art education, students are provided a range of opportunities to view and interpret artworks.*

examples from actual practice, those who use this book will be better equipped to implement the content and strategies suggested by the research.

Rethinking Curriculum in Art is meant to supplement, not replace, college-level curriculum texts that focus on the history and philosophy of curriculum and instruction. Such textbooks rarely enter into practical suggestions for curriculum design as we do here. In addition, throughout this book, we delineate important notions about curriculum planning in art education, which we hope will assist teachers in selecting and adopting art textbooks for their programs and districts. Such notions will provide those seeking to incorporate textbooks into their programs with the theoretical foundations necessary to make informed adoption decisions.

How This Book Is Organized

Chapter 2 begins with an overview of the theoretical context and school reform efforts within which the TETAC project and its curriculum guidelines were conceived and implemented. This chapter provides a conceptual context for developing curriculum to improve education and advance the arts as a part of the basic core learning in K–12 education. Here we examine ideas about art content and teaching that have emerged within education in general and arts education in particular. We review developments that have had an impact upon art curricula and look to current and emerging ideas about teaching and learning and, again, make connections between the ideas and arts curricula. Finally, drawing upon the work of those involved with the TETAC project, we introduce five key components of the curriculum design process.

Chapter 3 introduces the notion of "unit foundations"—the enduring ideas, key concepts, objectives, and plans for assessment and alignment with standards that need to be in place prior to designing

seek assistance in envisioning the larger picture— ways in which a range of art-teaching components work together as a curricular whole. To recognize the demand for this kind of assistance, one need only review e-mail requests to the discussion group ArtsEdnet Talk in recent years. Novice and seasoned teachers regularly ask for examples, templates, and other forms of assistance in district curriculum writing. This book will provide assistance for these efforts.

In addition to providing practical suggestions for curriculum writing, we draw heavily upon recent research findings. As such, we provide curriculum writers the necessary information to create substantive curricula consistent with current educational research. Because we include an extensive selection of instructional strategies and specific assessments. Units of study from TETAC project sites figure prominently here and in subsequent chapters.

We fully recognize the importance of making choices about artists, artworks, artifacts, cultures, and artmaking experiences, and in Chapter 4 we show how these significant decisions can be made in light of a larger conceptual framework, allowing teachers to identify and develop content consistent with the established unit foundations. In Chapter 5 we feature current and emerging ideas related to instruction and the ways in which students best learn. This material will help planners develop strategies to help students understand the enduring ideas and key concepts of their study units while developing proficiency in important inquiry processes.

Throughout the book we put forward the importance of planning assessment in the early, rather than later, stages of curriculum planning. Chapter 6 outlines specific approaches to conceiving and implementing assessment strategies to address the important ideas and skills established within unit foundations. Chapter 7 focuses on integrated, or interdisciplinary, curriculum planning, one of the important directions within the TETAC project and also in recent school reform efforts. We address integration among the arts as well as between art and other subject areas in the curriculum.

Finally, because we believe that any attempt to rethink curriculum in art must include attention to the impact of visual imagery in contemporary culture, Chapter 8 addresses visual culture, a focus of curriculum reform efforts that has received considerable attention since the conclusion of the TETAC project. Although the TETAC project did not directly address the importance of this subject area, we show how the approach to curriculum planning can accommodate an emphasis on visual culture. Our inclusion of this

chapter is consistent with our belief in the dynamic nature of curriculum. As new ideas take hold, we consider their relevance to our basic assumptions and make informed judgments regarding their inclusion within our curricula. While we recognize that some of the ideas in this text may one day surrender to new educational and social contexts that require different emphases and approaches, we trust that we have put forward, in this text and for today's readers, a compelling and useful approach for successfully rethinking curriculum in art.

1.3 Children take pride in the artworks they make. An important goal is to provide meaningful artmaking experiences for all students.

Chapter

2

Rethinking Curriculum in Context

"To raise new questions, new problems, to regard old problems from a new angle requires creative imagination and makes real advances. "
　—Albert Einstein

Since the 1960s, with the advent of the "arts as a discipline" movement, art educators have increasingly maintained that, in addition to providing opportunities for students to use materials and techniques for artistic expression, the teaching of art ought to provide opportunities for students to view and respond to artworks and understand the role of art in societies, past and present. In the 1980s these ideas coalesced in an approach to the teaching of the arts widely referred to as discipline-based arts education (DBAE). In the art curriculum, this approach drew upon the content and inquiry methods of the various disciplines of art history, art criticism, aesthetics, and artmaking or studio production as models for student engagement in an arts curriculum.

Looking Historically

The arts as a discipline movement originated in the early 1960s with the work of
Manual Barkan, an artist and educator
from the Department of Art Education at
Ohio State University. Barkan took his cue
from Jerome Bruner, a scientist who
responded to the national outcry over
Sputnik and the need to improve our
nation's schools by advocating curriculum
reform based on one major requirement:
Students should be given an understanding of the fundamental structure of a
discipline.[1]

2.1 TETAC teacher Hazel Lucas gathers her students
together to talk about an artwork.

One of the most important ideas associated with such
an expanded, or what some have called a "comprehensive," view of art curriculum content is that skills
in artmaking or art production are not viewed as the
sole or primary result of a student's experience in a
school-based art program. With this approach, students are to learn how the artistic expression of
humans throughout the world and over time has
served a range of purposes within societies. Students
are to be taught how to encounter and interpret the
meanings and/or messages of images, artifacts, and
performances, as well as to glean insight into their
own lives and the lives of others. In addition, students
are to be taught how to raise and address philosophical questions associated with images, artifacts, and
performances and our experiences with them.

In the mid-1980s, aligning itself with the arts as a
discipline movement and embracing a fourth area of
inquiry, aesthetics, along with the three areas identified by Barkan—art production, history, and criticism—the J. Paul Getty Trust opened the Getty Center
for Education in the Arts. Promoting DBAE, the Getty
advocated the arts as legitimate disciplines in their
own right, establishing regional institutes to spear-
head the movement. These institutes provided professional development and other services to teachers
throughout the country. Despite some initial contro-
versy, the arts education community eventually began
to embrace an expanded view of content in arts curricula and has slowly altered the image of arts education as just a "frill" in the minds of many policymakers,
educators, and parents.[2]

Art and the Human Experience: Shifting Assumptions

Changes in the approach to art curriculum have taken place within the context of shifts from modernist to postmodernist assumptions about art and the human experience. Along with this shift came a focus on artworks as having meaning and significance beyond the way in which they were organized—their form. Although the emphasis on an artwork's form is not synonymous with modernism, it is consistent with a modernist emphasis on universal ways to understand reality. The formalist view that, first and foremost, artworks are arrangements of elements of art according to certain principles has given way to a more contextualized understanding of artworks.

When placing an image or artifact within its original context, one begins to understand that artworks serve a range of purposes in society. It is not far from this realization to recognize that artworks take on different roles within different societies around the world and throughout time. Multiculturalism, with its recognition of the great diversity of human expression through art, has been embraced by the art education community, both in theory and in much of its practice. In addition, the art education community has recognized that art and its significance to cultural purpose can shift from one time period to another, from one group to another.

As the art curriculum content expanded to include art from other times and places and made for a variety of purposes, attention shifted from a primarily Western art historical perspective to a broader view of what we mean by art. In the K–12 curriculum, just as in art history programs within universities around the country, sole dependence upon traditional, Western "canons" of art was eschewed in favor of a much more inclusive curricular content. Images, objects, and performances made for a range of purposes in

Looking Historically

Manual Barkan's key points in proposing that the arts should be indispensable in the education of America's children included the following: Arts education could be conducted as a humanistic discipline.

- The structure of the arts exists in three domains— the productive, the historical, and the critical— each serving as a model for curriculum.

- Teaching should employ both problem-centered and discipline-centered strategies.

- Objectives and activities for learning in the arts should be developed through themes focused on life problems to allow for better integration with other subject areas.[3]

2.2 Teachers in a professional development workshop learn about the art and cultural traditions of India.

Looking Historically

As DBAE evolved, proponents felt that this approach

- provided for a rigorous and thorough understanding of any art form due to its focus on the four domains of study

- appealed not only to those students traditionally identified as gifted but to a wide range of thinkers and learners

- showed that artistic skills and understandings do not come automatically to students through exposure to the arts but must be nurtured and guided through the acquisition of artistic skills and perceptions

- showed that students' various stages of development and learning styles must be taken into consideration when designing learning experiences in the arts.[4]

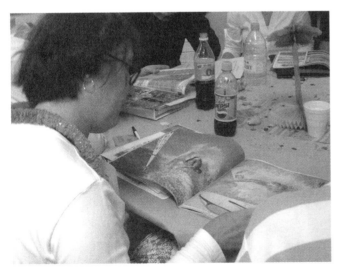

2.3 A teacher in a workshop focusing on visual culture explores media images related to surfing culture.

cultures around the globe and within our communities, past and present, were proposed as appropriate and desirable content for arts programs.

Close scrutiny of the roles that images play in contemporary life has given rise in recent years to calls for art education to focus attention on the power and importance of the visual in our global culture. Authors Marita Sturken and Lisa Cartwright, in the introduction to their book, *Practices of Looking: An Introduction to Visual Culture*, remind their readers that our culture ". . . has come to be dominated by visual rather than oral or textual media."[5] Art educators have championed the expansion of art education programs to include a serious examination of how images gain meaning in many cultural arenas. Sturken and Cartwright would agree, as evidenced in the following:

We are presented with a new set of challenges: to understand how images and their viewers make meaning, to determine what role images play in our cultures, and to consider what it means to negotiate so many images in our daily lives.[6]

With an emphasis on the cultural context of visual images—how images are presented and responded to in contemporary life—teachers can assist students in critically analyzing the way in which their ideas, beliefs, and behaviors are shaped through daily encounters with images in popular culture. Because the notion of visual culture has received so much attention in the art education community, it must be considered along with the other shifts in art education ideas, as we seriously rethink curriculum in art.

Evidence of these shifts in theory or ideas can be seen in the influx of commercially available teaching resources like art reproductions housed in posters, postcards, overhead transparencies, slides, videos, and, more recently, DVDs and CD-ROMs. Textbooks for use in K–12 art programs, too, evidence shifts in focus in the art curriculum. From textbooks that were organized around one studio project after another, textbooks now include historical and cultural information about artworks and prompts for students and teachers to interpret meanings found in artworks produced by others. In addition, some textbook programs are organized around themes and suggest links to other subject areas.[7]

An expanded view of art content, along with an increased number of resources available to teachers for addressing a comprehensive art education program, has resulted in art lessons that include critical viewing of and response to art and visual culture. Articles in magazines like *SchoolArts, Arts and Activities*, and *Art Education* have increasingly provided models for teachers to use in such lessons. To ensure that such activities are engaging for students, games and game-like strategies for developing abilities in critical response to art and visual culture have appeared in professional development workshops and materials offered by commercial vendors.[8]

Standards and the Rise of Assessment in the Arts

Another measure of the impact of a broadened view of art and how it is addressed in schools can be found in the arts standards at the national and state levels. In outlining what students should know and be able to do in the arts, the standards include reference to interpreting and judging artworks made by others and to knowing about the history of art in the Western and non-Western world. Again, the standards acknowledge the contexts in which artworks are created and perceived. Since their creation in 1994, the National Standards for the Arts have guided the development of curricula and curriculum resources.

2.4 *Former art teacher Stevie Mack recognized the need to provide materials to assist teachers in expanding their curricula to include a global perspective. She created her company, Crizmac, in 1986.*

Today, in school districts throughout the country, arts teachers are asked to ensure that the curricula they develop align with local, state, and national standards.

The creation of standards for learning in the arts and other subjects reinforced the need for assessment. Teachers were expected to determine the extent to which students learned what was intended for them to learn. Arts educators, along with educators in all fields, explored various structures and methods for assessing student achievement relative to the standards. For many art educators and for a variety of reasons, the area of assessment was new. Despite some teachers' initial resistance to the idea of assessment in art, art education has witnessed the develop-

Teachers in the TETAC project strove to have their students become responsible for their own learning. As they engaged students in discussions about artworks and philosophical issues, they were often surprised by their students' abilities. Consider the following from Janet Parker of Woodland High School, in Woodland, California:

"I was amazed by this [art criticism] lesson. It was by far the biggest surprise and one of the most pleasing days I have had as a teacher. I had that 'Aha!' moment while teaching this lesson. 'This is why I teach!' I planned the lesson to be thirty minutes or less, a kind of warm-up before I started something else. My surprise came when the discussion went on and on with intelligent and supported opinions from my wonderful students. The question of the day was: Is [Carmen Lomas] Garza's artwork as important as the great masterpieces? The response to this was great, from comments such as, 'Garza's art looks like it was made for a child's storybook,' to 'The *Mona Lisa* really has no importance because it doesn't say anything or have a deeper meaning.' Actual debates were respectfully going on and I just sat back amazed by the support my students were giving. I was also surprised by the other works of art the students brought into the discussions. If a student was not familiar with a piece of art, the student using it as an example would describe it in full detail. It was a beautiful day. The next day as the students were filing in and I was taking roll, I could still hear discussions going on."

ment of multiple methods for assessing student learning, including observations and dialogues, portfolios, performance tasks and projects, and traditional tests and quizzes.[9]

Under Construction: Conceptions of Student Learning

Reform efforts in education have also benefited from new understandings about how students learn. Educators recognize that, rather than being "given" or "delivered" by teachers, knowledge is constructed by the learner. Students are not viewed as receptacles for knowledge, coming to educational environments with clean slates to be filled by knowledgeable experts. Drawing upon the ideas of Dewey, Piaget, Vygotsky, and others, we have come to value the view that as students construct knowledge, learning is organized around the purposes of the learner, including social purposes, and occurs within cultural contexts as students use the cultural tools at hand to assist them in knowledge construction.[10]

Educators have also come to realize that identification of what students should know and be able to do, as prescribed by standards, is not the same as identifying those things that we wish students to *understand*. Understanding is a subtle and complex notion. To understand something goes beyond knowing or having a skill. Understanding implies having a certain degree of sophistication relative to a concept or topic, having the kinds of insights that can be demonstrated through a variety of performances and contexts. To teach for understanding is to provide opportunities for students ". . . to do a variety of thought-demanding things with a topic—like explaining, finding evidence and examples, generalizing, applying, analogizing, and representing the topic in a new way."[11] In addition to specific skills and certain knowledge that students should have, educators recognize that they must also teach for deep understanding of key concepts.

As we focus on assisting students to construct knowledge and deepen their understandings, we have come to value the importance of learners generating and addressing or investigating their own questions. Learning involves the use of metacognitive or reflective strategies on the part of the learner.[12] Educators recognize that with the assistance of knowledgeable adults, students need to be reflective learners, articulating what they know, what they want to learn, and how they might engage in learning.

2.5 Students are helped to reflect on their work in progress, making decisions about materials and techniques.

Making It Real and Making Connections

In order to generate and investigate their own questions, students need to see them as relevant to their own lives. In order for students to make meaning from their various encounters, they must be helped to integrate knowledge into their own lifeworlds.[13] We have recognized the importance of community involvement as parents and other community members interact with students and the curriculum. Students need to see the connection of school subject areas to the real world, but also that these subject areas are connected with one another. They need to see that in the world outside of school, people move through problems and construct knowledge through a wide range of interrelated content areas—not one at a time. Therefore, we have witnessed efforts to bring an interdisciplinary approach into the schools. These efforts propose to show how the arts are related in substantive ways to other subject areas.

As new understandings about the way students learn have been incorporated into the art curriculum, so, too, has recognition that assessment methods must follow suit. As reflective learners, students are encouraged to gauge their own progress toward learning goals. In recognizing the importance of tying knowledge construction to authentic, real-world engagement, educators have seen that assessment methods must also be relevant to the lives of students. Students are helped to apply their new understandings to life situations, to demonstrate their achievement through performance tasks and projects, often in contexts other than those strictly associated within the school.

Interdisciplinary Teaching and Learning

TETAC teachers were encouraged to design integrated units of study and thereby assist students in making substantive connections among concepts and skills in more than one subject area. The TETAC Curriculum Guidelines' focus on the importance of identifying enduring ideas and key concepts helped avoid the creation of superficial connections. Successful units tended to be those in which teachers articulated enduring ideas that crossed over several disciplines. To reinforce and deepen understanding of these ideas, teachers often selected specific artworks as a focus for interdisciplinary study.

A California fourth grade unit, for example, focused on the enduring idea, "all people tell stories to explain their world" (unit title: "Stories"; developed by Lynne Yamane, Carriage Elementary, Citrus Heights). The students examined two artworks, *The Creation* by contemporary artist Harry Fonseca and *Sunday Morning at the Mines* by nineteenth-century California artist Charles Christian Nahl. In very different ways, each of these artworks exemplifies the idea that stories are an important way for people to explain their world. Fonseca tells stories using symbols much like the petroglyphs and pictographs associated with his Native American heritage. Nahl's painting depicts life in the California gold mines during the Gold Rush era. In earth science lessons prior to their experiences with the artworks, students studied the layers of the earth, earthquakes, and various types of rocks and minerals as well as cave formations. During the study of caves, students learned about pictographs and petroglyphs made by Native Americans and others in California and places around the world.

Students had repeated opportunities to practice their skills in observing, describing, and interpreting the artworks, addressing both Visual Art and Language Arts standards. They compared and contrasted the two artworks in both oral and written form, paying particular attention to the way each artist told a story. Visual art and theater were integrated as students wrote and performed a Reader's Theater interpretation of the artworks.

Students read literature that featured stories about children living in California's past. Following a series of preparatory activities spaced throughout the unit, students created their own artworks in which they incorporated symbols to tell stories important to them.

Student understanding and appreciation of the artworks was deepened by their investigations of the social and historical contexts in which the artworks were made and to which they referred. Three field trips—one to a series of caverns, another to a reconstructed Native American village, and one to the site where gold was first found—provided opportunities for students to further deepen their understanding of social studies and science concepts while they experienced natural formations firsthand, and heard stories about people who lived and worked in the past. The students' substantive engagement with the artworks helped deepen their understanding of the enduring idea and key concepts of the unit.

Rethinking the Art Teacher's Role

The impact of shifts in our conceptions of how students learn on our conceptions of how teachers need to teach cannot be overemphasized. Add to this an expanded view of art content—what it is that students need to understand, know, and be able to do—and the challenge becomes even greater. If students learn best when they are encouraged to generate their own questions, engage in relevant investigations, and reflect upon their learning progress, then teachers need to develop strategies to provide opportunities for such substantive engagement. The role of the teacher must shift from that of one who dictates information to one who is a fellow inquirer as students construct knowledge. This shift has been characterized in popular educational talk as a shift from the teacher as "sage on the stage" to "guide on the side." While this appropriately characterizes an important change in the way teaching might be considered, and while this change is widely sanctioned by teachers as they talk about teaching outside of their classrooms, it is not an easy shift for most teachers to make when they return to those classrooms. For a variety of reasons, including those having to do with tradition, teacher confidence, a felt need for control, and typical school structures, teachers find it challenging, albeit important, to fully embrace this new role in classroom practice.

In courses devoted to teaching methodology and in professional development workshops and institutes, teachers have learned how to create engaging and enjoyable learning activities for students, often referred to as "hands-on" activities. Commercial resources and materials, again, are increasingly available to assist teachers in such efforts. However, inserting hands-on learning activities to address content is not alone sufficient for instruction that places the student in a central role for generating and investigating

Teacher Talk

In submitting their written units of instruction for evaluation, TETAC teachers routinely included reflections upon their work. In many of these reflections, teachers spoke of how important it was for them to articulate and teach toward the understanding of enduring ideas and key concepts. They often told of how they had been teaching a unit for many years, collecting related materials and designing interesting activities, but doing so without having a well-defined focus. The TETAC emphasis on identifying and teaching toward an understanding of enduring ideas and key concepts assisted them in structuring more meaningful and substantive units of study. Teachers became far more selective in choosing from an array of potential instructional strategies. Karen R. Gilmore of Clinton Elementary School, Lincoln, Nebraska, included the following in her reflection:

"The art of alignment in a unit is something I am now much more aware of. Do the key concepts guide the lessons? Are the art questions appropriate and do they fit with the artists and lesson design? Is the enduring idea an umbrella for lasting ideas that have value beyond the classroom? Is the art production in a lesson forced or is it a natural extension of the lesson? All of these questions and more help to define my passion for developing quality units that engage and excite students."

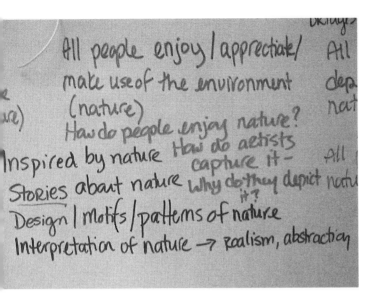

All people enjoy / appreciate / All
make use of the environment   dep.
(nature)   nat
How do people enjoy nature?
Inspired by nature How do artists
Stories about nature capture it — All
Why do they depict nature
it?
Design / Motifs / patterns of nature
Interpretation of nature → realism, abstraction

2.6 "Unpacking" the enduring idea through brainstorming, is a crucial step in the curriculum design process. Teachers often work together for this purpose.

questions tied to authentic interests and needs. Teachers are challenged to plan lessons that aim for deep understandings and avoid activity-driven instruction.

Drawing upon the recognition that much learning can be enhanced through interaction with one's peers, educators have implemented collaborative learning strategies, arranging students in groups and assigning roles for investigation. Again, as with hands-on activities, such group arrangements alone cannot represent a shift in the roles of the teacher and learners. Educators have found that while these pedagogical strategies represent valuable additions to traditional instruction, they must be accompanied by deliberate attempts to empower students to function as authentic inquirers and, accordingly, by a shift in

attitude and practice on the part of the teacher. In addition, they must be accompanied by a clear idea about their purpose relative to a set of clearly articulated and significant objectives.

Rethinking Curriculum: Choosing Wisely

Throughout these shifts in the assumptions at the core of teaching and learning, teachers are consistently asked to come together and write curriculum in their districts. They are given the task of ensuring that the curriculum is aligned with local, state, and national standards. More recently, they have also been required to ensure that the curriculum addresses content to ensure high test scores. Working alone, individual teachers, too, have sought ways to implement the changes in the way we think of art and art education, as well as new findings about teaching and learning.

To some extent, there is truth to the idea that teachers tend to teach what and how they were taught. We tend to hold on to old content and methods of instruction. Instead of taking stock and creating new curriculum from scratch, teachers may find it is often more expedient to merely match or "fit" tried and true content and approaches to standards or new mandates as they plan their curriculum.

The challenge in revisiting the process of curriculum planning is to take advantage of educational reform principles, draw upon important new understandings about teaching and learning, ground curriculum in broader conceptions of art, and carefully select from past practice only those things that make sense in light of these new understandings. Old practices, language, and vocabulary must be scrutinized for their relevance to important ideas, concepts, and skills.

The Enduring Idea as Firm Foundation

The TETAC Curriculum Guidelines Committee, guiding the development of units of instruction for implementation in the thirty-five partner schools, was charged with the responsibility of creating such guidelines to reflect the shifts that have taken place in our conceptions of art education, so that they would support a comprehensive approach to the study of art, attending to an expanded view of art that is multicultural and diverse. The guidelines also needed to take into account current understandings of how students learn best, how instruction and assessment need to be aligned with these understandings, and how the study of art should aim for a deep understanding of important or enduring ideas about art and the human experience.

To address their charge, the committee introduced the notion of using an "enduring idea" as the foundation for curriculum development. Enduring ideas comprise concepts that have drawn the attention of humans through the ages. The task force characterized enduring ideas as life issues that extend beyond specific disciplines and that have lasting human importance. "The inner quest for self-knowledge," "the relationships between humans and nature," and "the relationships among humans" are examples of such enduring ideas because they allow subject areas, including the arts, to be developed in substantive ways. These enduring ideas function in both generative and delimiting ways. In developing a unit of instruction based upon enduring ideas, unit writers delineate key concepts and provocative questions to further the exploration of the ideas. The enduring ideas, key concepts, and questions provide the impetus and focus for the development of instruction throughout the unit and are reiterated within each of the unit's lessons.

Teacher Talk

Teachers involved in the TETAC project were asked to rethink the way they had designed curriculum in the past. Notes Lois Rongisch of Tara Heights Elementary School, Papillion, Nebraska, in reflecting upon her work with the TETAC Curriculum Guidelines that required early identification of the enduring ideas, key concepts, and evidence for assessment (called "unit foundations"):

"The study of these foundations has changed the way I put together, even think about, curriculum. In the past, I felt I had good lessons. But after going through this process, I can see that they had a 'disconnected connection.' Using this format, I have been able to pull together ideas in a more meaningful unit and align them with successful child-centered activities that meet the objectives. Thus, the children better understand the lessons and activities and the connections they have with one another. I have seen many 'ahas' from the children while doing this unit. The students were very enthusiastic about participating in these lessons, and the questioning techniques this process employs challenges them and raises their thinking level a notch or two."

2.7 When students are aware of the enduring ideas, key concepts, and objectives in a unit, they know what they are responsible for learning and frequently want to share their new knowledge with others.

In the TETAC project, professional development at the local and national levels was designed to assist teachers in developing the conceptual foundations to frame and shape curriculum content and to align instruction and assessment tasks and performances to these foundational ideas, concepts, and questions. The guidelines also explained how these foundations could help teachers meet local, state, and national standards. The guidelines emphasized that by using enduring ideas and other foundational components, a teacher could avoid activities insignificant for lifelong learning.

Teachers at the thirty-five TETAC partner schools worked with the guidelines to create units of instruction to be taught in grades K–12. Most of these units were integrated or interdisciplinary, but all units included one or more of the arts as a significant focus. All included a focus on enduring ideas as well as strategies for instruction and assessment that reflect our emerging understandings of how students best learn.

The Curriculum Development Process

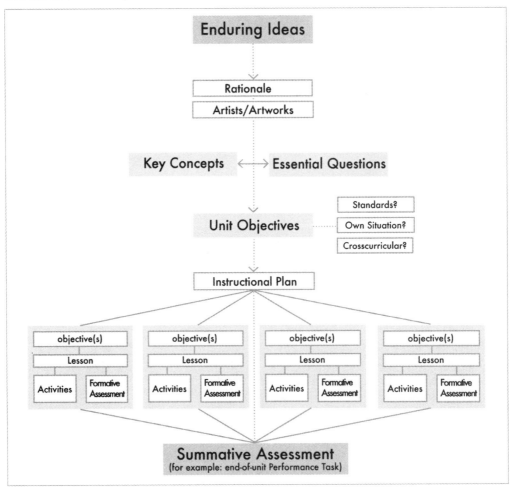

The Big Five: Key Components of the Development Process

The TETAC Curriculum Task Force delineated five components of the curriculum development process—Unit Foundations, Content, Instruction, Assessment, and Design. These components were not necessarily seen as sequential steps to be taken, except in the case of the unit foundation, which, because it involves identifying the enduring ideas upon which the unit is to based, was seen as paramount in curriculum design. Once the enduring idea is established, the work of identifying key concepts, essential questions, instruction, and assessment occurs in a variety of ways, usually nonlinear, allowing for collaboration among curriculum planners and a certain degree of trial and error, and accommodating the intuitive nature of such an endeavor. What follows here is a brief description of the components as delineated in the TETAC project final report.[14]

Unit Foundations

This area defines the foundations for integrating inquiry across disciplines and aligning all components of a unit, including assessment, content, and instruction. Key to the unit foundations is the establishment of an enduring idea around which inquiry in the arts and other disciplines can be meaningfully integrated. These ideas are not discipline-specific but embrace life issues that have lasting human importance and appear to be of continual concern to humans at different times and in different cultures. These ideas are explored repeatedly through the perspectives offered by the various disciplines.

Content

This area outlines the knowledge and skills to be introduced or developed in exploring the enduring idea, including the alignment of local curriculum standards and mandates. In the visual arts, knowledge and skills are drawn from four domains—art history, aesthetics, art production, and criticism.

Instruction

This area guides teachers in planning the learning strategies to use in delivering the unit. Instruction is primarily, though not exclusively, based on student-centered, inquiry-based teaching approaches to help students arrive at an understanding of the enduring idea.

Assessment

This area guides teachers in structuring and aligning assessment activities with the enduring idea and the unit content to make sure that the learning activities are relevant and engaging.

2.8 A curator shows teachers the original artwork that will feature prominently in a unit they are creating.

Design

This area outlines criteria for teachers to use in reviewing the quality of a whole unit of instruction to ensure that the areas of the unit are aligned and coherent and that the sequencing of lessons and the relationships among concepts are clear.

Many curriculum writers in the TETAC project employed the process of working with what writers Grant Wiggins and Jay McTighe call "backward design."[15] This approach consists of first identifying enduring ideas, key concepts, and essential questions, then articulating what would count as acceptable evi-

dence that students understand and are able to perform in the outlined ways, and only then designing instructional strategies to move students toward the desired ends. The authors refer to this approach as "backward" because it represents a departure from the common practice of planning instruction prior to assessment. The remaining chapters of this book highlight and explore in more depth each of the TETAC Curriculum Development Components, with examples from units planned by teachers in the project prominently featured.

Lessons Learned

The TETAC project held high expectations for students, including that they

- actively construct knowledge, rather than passively receive knowledge

- pursue understanding, not simply memorize and reproduce knowledge

- engage in developing contextualized meanings, not learn isolated facts

- develop self-awareness as learners

The TETAC project expected that curriculum would include

- integrated/interdisciplinary learning

- group planning

- utilization of technology

- writing through the curriculum

- collaborative learning

- representation of global and local topics/issues

- new forms of student assessment

- community-based content

- local control over curriculum

The TETAC project expected that assessment would be authentic, with assessment tasks that ask students to

- construct rather than reproduce knowledge

- consider alternative solutions, strategies, and perspectives

- employ ideas and theories central to academic and professional disciplines

- utilize writing to demonstrate understanding

- examine problems or issues found in life beyond the classroom

- demonstrate understanding for an audience beyond the teacher, classroom, or school

Source: The National Arts Education Consortium, "Goals and Expectations for the Transforming Education Through the Arts Challenge," February 26, 1999.

Notes

1   National Arts Education Consortium, *Transforming Education Through the Arts Challenge: Final Project Report* (Columbus, OH: The Ohio State University, Department of Art Education, n.d.), p. 13.

2   Ibid., p. 18.

3   Ibid., pp. 14–15.

4   Ibid., p. 17.

5   M. Sturken and L. Cartwright, *Practices of Looking: An Introduction to Visual Culture* (New York: Oxford University Press, 2001), p. 1.

6   Ibid.

7   See, for example, *Art and the Human Experience,* a three-volume middle-school textbook series authored by Eldon Katter and Marilyn Stewart, Davis Publications (www.davis-art.com).

8   See, for example, *Token Response, Artery, Philosophy and Art,* and *Artifacts,* by Eldon Katter and Mary Erickson, published by Crizmac Art and Cultural Education Materials, Inc. (www.crizmac.com).

9   See, for example, D. Beattie, *Assessment in Art Education* (Worcester, MA: Davis Publications, 1997).

10 A. Efland, *Art and Cognition: Integrating the Visual Arts in the Curriculum* (New York: Teachers College Press, 2002; Reston, VA: National Art Education Association), pp. 80–81.

11 D. Perkins and T. Blythe, "Putting Understanding Up Front," *Educational Leadership* 51, no. 5 (1994), pp. 5–6.

12 A. Elfland, *Art and Cognition,* p. 81.

13 Ibid.

14 National Arts Education Consortium, *Transforming Education Through the Arts Challenge: Final Project Report,* p. 28.

15 G. Wiggins and J. McTighe, *Understanding by Design* (Alexandria, VA: Association for Supervision and Curriculum Development, 1998), p. 8.

Making It Count: Unit Foundations

"Let the main ideas which are introduced into a child's education be few and important, and let them be thrown into every combination possible."
—Philosopher Alfred North Whitehead

Spread over the bright white tablecloths of the Ohio State University Faculty Club ballroom were images of Maya Lin's renowned Vietnam Veterans Memorial, sited in Washington, D.C.; Jacob Lawrence's bold portrait of the freedom fighter Harriet Tubman; a magazine cover shot of basketball superstar Michael Jordan; ceramicist Robert Arneson's satirical depiction of Mona Lisa and George Washington; and photomontage artist Barbara Kruger's untitled representation of a 1950s pigtailed young girl admiring the flexed muscles of her young male companion accompanied by the text "We don't need another hero." How could the art teachers, classroom teachers, and art education professors gathered around the ballroom tables bring coherence to this disparate array of images, ones that crossed boundaries of time, media, visual form, and function?

Two questions—what is a hero and why do we need heroes—drew these divergent works together, revealing conceptual connections among the images that were not initially apparent. Through the multiple images, the idea of the hero was revealed in its complexity, prompting lively discussions about how heroes are defined, redefined, changed, and at times challenged.

Although engaging, the larger purpose of these deliberations extended beyond considerations of heroes. The art and classroom teachers were learning about a curriculum approach focused on the use of enduring ideas. Teachers may often relate and refer to this notion as a thematic approach that has frequently characterized study in the humanities.

In this chapter, we focus on what it means to construct art curriculum with enduring ideas as a foundation. We address such questions as What are the philosophical and educational implications of framing curriculum with enduring ideas? Why endorse enduring ideas for arts curriculum? What happens to arts content when enduring ideas are foundational? and How do these notions relate to current educational theory and practice? In our discussion we include examples from the TETAC project as a way of demonstrating how enduring ideas look in classroom practice.

3.1 Barbara Kruger, Untitled, 1987. Photographic silkscreen/vinyl photomontage, 109" x 210" (272.5 x 525 cm). Courtesy of Mary Boone Gallery, New York.

3.2 *TETAC teachers interpreting artworks about the enduring idea of heroes.*

Enduring Ideas and Curriculum Foundations

Curriculum design is highly involved with decision making about inclusions and exclusions. Philosophical and conceptual commitments, not always overtly articulated, underlie curriculum design and influence how education is shaped. In our approach, choosing enduring ideas as a foundation for curriculum represents a philosophical commitment to content that exceeds any one subject matter or discipline.[1] Enduring ideas such as identity, justice, relationships, interdependence, survival, power, humans and nature, conflict, celebration, freedom, emotions, and spirituality are not owned, so to speak, by the arts, history, science, math, or any of the school subjects. Such ideas have educational import because they link academic subject matter with life-focused issues. The Ohio State TETAC faculty's support for enduring ideas amplifies this perspective. They explain:

[W]hen educators shift from a dominant discipline-based orientation to a focus on "real life" issues,

Enduring Ideas Defined

Enduring ideas are similar to themes, topics, or issues that reflect big questions about the human experience and have been investigated over time. They are broad, umbrella-like ideas that guide students in understanding what it means to be human, to live alongside others and in the natural world. Here are some examples:

identity

survival

power

conflict

spirituality

relationships

humans and nature

reality and fantasy

life and death

interdependence

good and evil

life cycles

rites of passage

change

ritual

problems, and skills, students will find their learning more meaningful and will be more active participants in it. This enhances the making of connections and in-depth understanding of concepts, and it promotes mastery of the knowledge and skills that prepare students for life in today's world.[2]

Enduring ideas may be expressed in single terms, such as "identity," but they may also be more expansively stated as "all people, regardless of time and place, are searching for personal identity." Or in another example, an enduring idea about celebration might be expressed as a single term or more elaborately as "over time, humans have created celebrations to mark significant life events." No matter how an enduring idea is stated, what is most important is the subsequent conceptual development of the idea for instruction. The latter portion of this chapter delves into this development with a discussion and examples of "unpacking" enduring ideas with key concepts and essential questions.

Enduring Ideas in Context

In the TETAC project, flexibility was an important aspect of enduring ideas because they were required to be useful in a variety of contexts. From personal experiences and those with the TETAC project, we found enduring ideas to be highly adaptable to diverse age levels, specific student populations, and a variety of educational contexts. For example, in the TETAC project in a Nebraska high school, English students investigated identity as an enduring idea by examining the lives of nineteenth-century midwestern pioneer teenagers and adults during the 1930s in a Willa Cather novel and several Grant Wood paintings. In the TETAC project in a Texas high school English class, students from a large Hispanic population explored the enduring idea of identity by reading contemporary novelist Sandra Cisneros's *The House on*

Mango Street, a compilation of poetic vignettes about growing up in Chicago as a Mexican-American, and by interpreting contemporary artist Carmen Lomas Garza's paintings revealing her Mexican and Spanish heritage.[3] Although one school taught the enduring idea by using a writer and artist from the past while the other school used a contemporary writer and artist, the enduring idea and concepts related to identity were similar in both of these high school curriculum units. In both instances, the students studied an enduring idea through a context that had specific relevance for their own lives. These two examples and others exemplify how enduring ideas apply to specific contexts and circumstances. This should not be surprising, since enduring ideas represent human concerns that have been of significance over time in multiple cultures and contexts.

Enduring Ideas and Age Level

Are enduring ideas appropriate for elementary students? Would it be better to design elementary curriculum foundations around other concerns? Our experiences and anecdotal reports from elementary teachers suggest that success in teaching enduring ideas at the elementary level is a matter of conceptualizing enduring ideas in an accessible manner. Elementary students would not pursue enduring ideas at the same conceptual or abstract level as older students, nor for that matter, would lower-level elementary students engage an enduring idea in the same manner as upper-level elementary students.

In the TETAC project we witnessed the use of enduring ideas at all elementary age levels. Lower-elementary students simply did not consider enduring ideas in as abstract terms. For example, the enduring idea of relationships is commonly taught at the lower elementary level in terms of family, friends, and community. These topics may not usually

FAQs

How do I begin?

One might say that selecting an enduring idea is the starting point for curriculum design, but that is not always practical or realistic. More often, curriculum design begins elsewhere—with the choice of artists or artworks for study, a particular curriculum objective, an artmaking medium, specific student interests, or a schoolwide event. In such cases, selecting enduring ideas occurs within these parameters. In the following example, the enduring idea of "The Social World" was derived after the selection of an artwork, Georges Seurat's noted painting *A Sunday on La Grande Jatte* (1884).

Finding an Enduring Idea in an Artwork

The leadership team at Fair Elementary, an Ohio TETAC school, chose Seurat's large pointillist painting *La Grande Jatte* as their focus for a schoolwide theme. Many of the teachers were familiar with this painting from the Art Institute of Chicago , and one of the TETAC mentors had previously conducted considerable research about it. A topiary garden, designed to evoke Seurat's pointillist painting and located in a nearby park that students could visit, provided another frame of reference for students. Thus the teachers on the leadership team found several good reasons for developing curriculum units around this artwork.

La Grande Jatte is often studied in K–12 classrooms as an example of Seurat's pointillistic technique, in which the artist applies colors to the canvas in small dots. But there is much more to understand about Seurat's work than simply his painting technique. The selection of an enduring idea was essential in deepening the study of this artwork beyond a study of a Postimpressionist painting technique or even the portrayal of a leisurely Sunday afternoon in the park. The leadership team's selection of "Our Social World" as the enduring idea allowed the painting to become a focus for student investigation into questions about society, both French nineteenth-century society and their own contemporary social world. The following essential questions, which guided the unit, were formulated for the purpose of exploring this enduring idea:

> *What is a social world?*
> *How does the social world influence your values and beliefs?*
> *What causes the social world to change?*

The enduring idea of the social world extended student learning beyond nineteenth-century French society to a more comprehensive understanding of the world as a social place as they identified various social roles and relationships in the painting, ideas that were extended to their own social world.

Enduring Ideas and Related Topics Employed by Nebraska TETAC Art and Classroom Teachers

- *Enduring Idea:* Interdependence
  Related Topic: Wetlands, "A Story of Interdependence"
  Mark Lago, grade 4–5 classroom teacher Clinton Elementary School

- *Enduring Idea:* Conflict
  Related Topic: Personal Experiences
  Angie Piontek, grade 4–5 classroom teacher Clinton Elementary School

- *Enduring Idea:* Cooperation
  Related Topic: Human relationships, "Build Bridges, Not Walls"
  Jody Jansky, special-education teacher, Clinton Elementary School

- *Enduring Idea:* Survival
  Related Topic: Humans and the Environment
  Heather Nebesniak, grade 3 classroom teacher, Valley Elementary School

- *Enduring Idea:* Identity
  Related Topic: Self-identity, "The Search for Identity"
  Josette Kluck, English teacher, Columbus High School

- *Enduring Idea:* Social Power
  Related Topic: Symbols, "The Persuasive Power of the Visual Environment"
  Jan Jones, art teacher, Kearney Elementary School

- *Enduring Idea:* Survival
  Related Topic: Humans and the Environment
  Heather Nebesniak, grade 3 classroom teacher, Clinton Elementary School

- *Enduring Idea:* Power
  Related Topic: "The Individual and the Group"
  Candace Becher, English teacher, Clinton Elementary School

be conceptualized in terms of an enduring idea of relationships, but they are familiar topics to the elementary curriculum. Placing family, friends, and community under the enduring idea of relationships provides greater connections for these topics, strengthening the potential for learning. It is the connections that students make between bits of knowledge that develop deeper understandings and avoid the pitfall of simply piling up more and more facts.[4] Thus, providing a large overall idea for linking several different topics offers students a strong conceptual learning tool. The enduring ideas of identity, justice, relationships, interdependence, survival, power, humans and nature, conflict, celebration, freedom, emotions, and spirituality would not be remote or distant from elementary students if taught with topics within their realm of experience. The following examples of fourth graders who studied the enduring idea of identity demonstrate this point.

In preparation for composing and performing an opera about community and identity, fourth-grade students in Cleveland studied and compared painter Carmen Lomas-Garza's paintings depicting a Mexican-American community with artist Faith Ringgold's portrayal of an African-American community in her story quilts. The classroom teacher, Ms. Doering, comments, "It was interesting to watch the students make connections between their culture and those of Faith and Carmen."[5]

In this same Cleveland elementary school, another fourth-grade class studied identity from a personal perspective by reading Vincent van Gogh's letters to his brother Theo. The art teacher, Ms. Pittard, followed this experience by having the students create self-portraits to include in a letter to someone in their family.[6] These fourth graders studied the same enduring idea, identity, as the Nebraska and Texas high school students previously described, and in one instance, the same artist. No doubt the high school and elementary discussions about identity engendered different questions, concepts, and concerns; but the enduring idea had relevance both for the teenagers and the nine- and ten-year-olds.

Our approach to curriculum design encompasses not only discipline knowledge and ways of knowing but also contextual approaches. That is, we frame the discipline knowledge and processes of the arts with enduring ideas. With this approach, life-focused issues

3.3 Lyrics from opera created by fourth graders at Newton D. Baker Elementary School for the Arts, Cleveland, Ohio, Ms. Gloria Doering, teacher

The following comments derive from art teachers who participated in a university course, "Designing Art Curriculum," which focused instruction around big ideas—another name for enduring ideas.

• Louis Tiberi, middle school art teacher

"I have always tried to have my students make their work meaningful for themselves, but I never really gave them any strategies to do so. By using a big idea and taking into consideration my students' knowledge base, I feel I can more effectively design artmaking problems."

• Andrew Moffatt, elementary art teacher

"I know I was aware that artists had big ideas, but I was not really focused on how they got those ideas. I was mostly operating on the outdated 'artist as genius' model that I had conceptually rejected years ago. . . . I suppose I had assumed artists' ideas were innate and not a process that they worked through. . . . By chance I heard [artist Chuck] Close in a radio interview in which he expressed how he was thankful he didn't have to come up with a new idea for each painting."

• Kathy Gaynor, elementary art teacher

"The big idea was a new perspective for curriculum design for me. I always include a theme, but a big idea goes deeper into the heart of artmaking."

• Linda Jackson, elementary art teacher

"I want to guide students . . . so they understand the 'whole picture' of artmaking—the skills and the meaning. . . . I think this really means a change in approach on my part, a shift in focus. The elementary youngsters do need to learn skills and techniques so they are able to express themselves creatively. I'm thinking, now, that I can teach the skills and tie the artmaking to a big idea."

How do I begin?

Finding an Enduring Idea in a School Event

A TETAC mentor at a Nebraska middle school utilized an annual recognition breakfast for graduating eighth graders as the impetus to design a unit of study around the enduring idea of identity.

> *"The recognition ceremony serves as the culminating activity for what has been a transitional year for students. The eighth grade stands between childhood and young adulthood. Social scientists refer to these transitional events as rites of passage. These events mark important stages in our lives and give us the opportunity to reflect on our accomplishments and ourselves. It is the self-reflective nature of the year-end recognition ceremony that provided the impetus for designing a unit about identity. . . . During this unit of study, I want students to not only reflect on who they are, but also on the nature of identity itself as they examine how art can express identity."[7]*

Linking units of study to real-life occasions, when possible, provides an important connection between academic learning and life outside the classroom.

are examined, interpreted, and explored through ways of knowing derived from art criticism, artmaking, aesthetics, and art history. Does such an approach diminish art content? Sydney Walker and Michael Parson argue that focusing art curriculum around human issues does not relinquish what is valuable about the arts, but presents "more of an opportunity to capitalize on exactly what makes the arts powerful and significant, their ability to convey the complexity and ambiguity of human values, beliefs, interpretations about life."[8] Often arts learning has been divorced from life with technical skills, formal elements, media, and historical styles assuming an independent significance bereft of a meaningful reference to larger schemes of meaning.

Why Frame Visual Arts Learning with Enduring Ideas?

Bethany Rogers argues that often school subjects lack "the animating factors that characterize a disciplinary field, the process of inquiry and building knowledge.[9] The 1960s curriculum reform movement led by Jerome Bruner sought to strengthen schooling through a focus upon discipline structures, constructing knowledge as ways of knowing rather than a factual body of knowledge to be absorbed. As Rogers and others recognize, often school subjects are not taught in this manner. It appears that subject matter often continues to be taught as a body of inert knowledge for dissemination rather than a dynamic set of discipline processes and principles to be appropriated for active exploration and making sense of the world.

Chapter 4, "Making Choices: Selecting Lesson Content to Build on Unit Foundations," approaches arts content through art criticism, art history, aesthetics, and artmaking. The attempt is to engage students with the inquiry processes associated with these various areas. Why then do we need enduring ideas? We respond by citing curriculum theorist Ralph Tyler's argument that while curriculum reform of the 1960s stressed disciplinary structures, it gave insufficient attention to the needs and interests of the learner.[11] This complaint, a common critique of the 1960s curriculum reforms, reminds us of Dewey's admonition to seek a balance between subject area content and student needs and interests. The marriage of visual arts subject matter with enduring ideas that have relevance and significance for students' present and future lives offers opportunities for achieving this equilibrium.

In one of the previous curriculum examples, fourth graders created self-portraits and wrote letters to their families. Central discipline principles, cogent to understandings of the artmaking process, informed this lesson. In creating their self-portraits, the fourth graders learned that artmaking is purposeful and can be an occasion to explore ideas for further meanings. Framing the fourth graders' artmaking with the enduring idea of identity provided a vehicle for the students to engage these fundamental artmaking principles. Their artmaking was purposeful and an opportunity to learn more about themselves and who they are. Without this enduring idea, the fourth graders may not have encountered these artmaking principles. Their self-portraits might have become exercises in developing technical skills of representation rather than an opportunity to explore and investigate an important idea.

In another previous curriculum example, Texas high school students interpreted the paintings of Mexican-American artist Carmen Lomas Garza, exercising an important art criticism principle that views artworks as symbolic objects. The high school students could have interpreted Lomas Garza's works with symbolic meanings without framing them within a study

FAQs

What if enduring ideas are too abstract for instruction?

This is where a unit topic can become useful. In our experience, teachers usually need to identify a specific topic for teaching an enduring idea. For example, the enduring idea of humans and nature is quite broad and would require identifying a specific topic to focus a study of this idea. Students might learn about humans and nature through a study of ecosystems, weather, urban renewal projects, or gardens.

of identity. So what did the enduring idea of identity contribute to the students' learning? Ms. Parker, the English teacher who created the unit, states that the students worked in small groups to investigate one of Lomas Garza's paintings with a specific question. Afterward the high school students participated in a whole-group discussion about the meaning of the artworks. Rather than concluding the activity at this point, Ms. Parker enlarged the discussion to explore the concept of cultural identity, how it can be recognized in Lomas Garza's work, and how cultural identity manifests itself in the students' school and classroom environment. In this example, the enduring idea provided a focus not only for interpreting Lomas Garza's work, but for connecting the discussion ideas to the students own lives.

Making Curriculum Choices for Relevance and Diversity

Curriculum design is inherently about choices. The criteria we employ for making curriculum choices is very simple: a concern for both relevance and diversity. In regard to relevance, we have three areas in mind: (1) student interests and needs, (2) artistic understandings and processes, and (3) contemporary culture. Thus, the choice of an enduring idea, artist, artwork, or culture for study should be guided by consideration of the relationship to the students' interests, needs, and future lives; the potential to engage specific art understandings and artistic-inquiry processes; and the instance of meaningful connections to contemporary culture.

Diversity as a criterion for curriculum choices refers to an awareness of the range of possibilities in a particular area regarding ideas, issues, themes, artists, artworks, artifacts, or cultures to be studied. Diversity does not serve the curriculum well as a stand-alone criterion. That is, including a culture, artist, or media simply for the purpose of being inclusive can result in a curricular hodge-podge rather than in meaningfully constructed learning. Obviously the curriculum cannot include all artists, artworks, cultures, skills, techniques, ideas, and issues, but it is wise to consider the range of possibilities when making curriculum choices, striving particularly for a curriculum configuration that makes sense in terms of the three areas we identified for relevance in making curriculum choices.

Developing Unit Foundations for Instruction

The steps in the process of designing curriculum foundations have been carefully considered and implemented with numerous teachers at the elementary, middle school, and high school levels who have found them highly useful. A third-grade Nebraska teacher remarks about this process, "In the past, I felt I had good lessons. But after going through this process, I can see that they had a 'disconnected connection.' Using this format, I have been able to pull together ideas in a more meaningful unit."[12]

There are no hard-and-fast rules for creating unit foundations with enduring ideas, but the following demonstrates what the process might look like.

1. Getting Started

An entire school may select an enduring idea or a single teacher, grade level, or subject area department may select an enduring idea for a unit of study. Enduring ideas can direct an entire course of study, a single unit, or an entire curriculum.

2. Choosing the Enduring Idea

Select an enduring idea with the following criteria in mind.

- What is the importance of the idea? Is it worth studying?
- What is the appropriateness of the idea for students? How does it relate to their present and future interests and needs?
- How does it relate to contemporary culture?
- How is the enduring idea represented in the arts?

3. Writing a Rationale

Explain why the enduring idea is important for learning and for your students in particular. See the sidebar on page 34 for an example of how a rationale might be constructed.

4. "Unpacking" the Enduring Idea: Key Concepts First

Once an enduring idea has been selected and validated with a rationale, what is the next step? To become useful, enduring ideas must be further developed. Unpacking the concepts of an enduring idea will reveal what it is about from diverse perspectives. Although you will find that essential questions, which we will talk about shortly, are useful for directing instruction, it is a mistake to skip over developing key concepts. When you move directly from an enduring idea to essential questions, often you do not have the needed depth and understanding of an enduring idea. Key concepts can be the intermediate step between an enduring idea and the essential questions that develop this depth of understanding.

To begin the development of key concepts, we've found it's almost always a good idea to start by brainstorming key concepts that explain what the enduring idea is about. Think about what is implied by the idea, considering diverse perspectives. Then create a list of at least twelve to twenty key concepts that might be associated with the enduring idea.

As an example, here is a list of key concepts for the enduring idea "Communication is an essential aspect of what it means to be human."

- Communication can be verbal and nonverbal.
- Communication requires interpretation.
- Communication can be public and private.
- Communication can be direct or indirect.
- Communication can be misunderstood.
- Communication can be literal or symbolic.
- Communication is about style as well substance.
- Communication requires a form of language.
- Communication is essential for survival.
- Communication can persuade.
- Communication invokes response.
- Communication creates dialogue.
- Communication informs.
- Communication evolves.
- Communication requires interaction.
- Communication can be formal or informal.

Now, what to do with this list? The purpose of a brainstorming list is to generate as many concepts as possible, but at some point you need to synthesize and select those ideas that seem most important. Often several key concepts can be collapsed into a single concept. Select the concepts that will be significant for the unit. You will use these concepts later in developing unit and lesson objectives.

As you consider your list of key concepts, certain ones should stand out as significant. Prioritize those concepts for instructional emphasis. For example, from the previous list the following concepts appear to indicate significant issues.

- Communication requires interpretation.
- Communication can be public and private.
- Communication can be misunderstood.
- Communication can be literal or symbolic.
- Communication is about style as well as substance.
- Communication is essential for survival.
- Communication can persuade.

The key concept "communication requires interpretation" raises an important issue that indicates the complexity and difficulty of communication. This issue is also implied in other key concepts, such as "communication can be literal or symbolic" and "communication can be misunderstood." Another intriguing issue is suggested by the concept "communication can be both private and public." This raises possible questions about the different uses of communication and how they affect communication.

Other concepts might be considered less important in that they reflect more literal or obvious ideas, such as "communication informs" or "communication invokes response."

Further, a list of key concepts usually reveals redundancies that can be combined and collapsed or eliminated. It is important to create a meaningful list of

FAQs

Why do I need a rationale?

Writing a rationale permits you to explain why a particular enduring idea has instructional relevance for your students. It motivates you to examine whether or not the idea is worth teaching and if it is appropriate for the intended students. Further, it initiates thinking about what is significant about the idea and what should be the focus of instruction.

What does a rationale look like?

Example: A unit based on the enduring idea of humans and nature.

The Rationale

Why is this enduring idea important for my students to learn about?

In studying contemporary life in relationship to nature, my urban students can develop an awareness of the gap that exists between contemporary society and direct experiences with nature. By interpreting and investigating the work of conceptual artist James Turrell and installation artist Sandy Skoglund, students can learn that contemporary artists address the subject of human interaction with nature from different perspectives, and by examining their own lives they can consider the enduring idea from a personal perspective. Studying humans and nature from multiple perspectives such as these can provide a basis for students to question the relationship of humans and nature in a contemporary context.

How long should I make my rationale?

One or two paragraphs should be extensive enough. You want to get to the point of why the enduring idea is generally important to teach and more specifically important for your students.

3.4 Teachers can work together as they brainstorm concepts related to an enduring idea. Here, a group of teachers is mapping the enduring idea of identity.

key concepts, not simply a long list. One other helpful hint about creating key concepts is to make sure that all of the concepts begin with the same sentence stem, "Communication is . . ." Repetition of a single sentence stem for the key concepts organizes your thinking, allowing you to more easily compare and contrast the concepts.

5. Formulating Essential Questions

Essential questions synthesize key concepts and bring focus to the unit. Think about it. A unit with a number of different lessons can easily veer into many diverse directions. What will keep instruction on track? The enduring idea is a broad focus, but there is a need for more specific direction. The key concepts are useful, but they may represent too many ideas to keep in mind at once. As the instructor of a unit, you should be able to remind yourself and students of the central learning purposes for a unit without having to consult a written plan. The essential questions serve this function. They fall in between the generality of the enduring idea and the specificity of key concepts. Each essential question can encompass a number of key concepts.

Examples of essential questions for the previous communication example might include:

- What counts as communication?
- Why is communication often difficult?
- Why is communication important?

These essential questions incorporate key concepts from the previous list. For example, the first essential question, "What counts as communication?" incorporates concepts such as communication can be verbal and nonverbal, communication can be public and private, communication is about style as well as substance, and communication requires a form of language. The second essential question, "Why is

communication often difficult?" relates to concepts such as communication must be interpreted, communication can be literal or symbolic, and communication can be misunderstood. And the third essential question, "Why is communication important?" suggests the key concepts that communication is essential for survival and communication can be persuasive.

As this example of essential-question forming shows, it is easier to keep a short list of essential questions about communication in mind than it is to recall a long list of key concepts. As students and teachers raise the essential questions throughout a unit, they should trigger recollection of the key concepts and other concepts as well.

That's right. Essential questions are for students as much as teachers in guiding exploration of an enduring idea. Essential questions also provide teachers with an assessment tool. If students know that the essential questions will become a major factor in assessing their understanding at the conclusion of the unit, students can use them to focus their learning during the unit. Having too many essential questions defeats the purpose of synthesizing and focusing the unit content. For this reason, they should be limited to no more than three, and sometimes even a single essential question might be sufficient to bring focus to a unit. And one more thing: keep in mind, as you write essential questions, that you want to engage students while, at the same time, motivating them to think beyond their usual frames of reference.

6. Inserting Unit Objectives

You now have an enduring idea, key concepts, and essential questions. Is there more to the unit foundations? Yes, just a few more steps. At this point, it is a good idea to insert the unit objectives to identify what students will understand or be able to do (skills) as a result of their engagement in this unit of study.

Are unit objectives the same as lesson objectives? No. Just as essential questions are broader than lesson questions, unit objectives are also more comprehensive than lesson objectives. A unit might only have a few unit objectives, but more objectives for specific lessons within the unit. Remember, at this stage of unit development—the establishment of unit foundations—you should be thinking broadly.

Unit objectives are a restatement, in a general way, of the enduring idea, key concepts, and essential questions you've identified.

For example, continuing with the communication unit example, the following would be unit objectives.

- Students will understand why communication is important to human life.
- Students will understand what counts as communication.
- Students will understand why communication is often difficult.
- Students will understand why communication is important personally and socially.
- Students will understand how and why communication can be interpreted.

You might note that the first three unit objectives are merely a restatement of the essential questions: What counts as communication? Why is communication often difficult? and Why is communication important?

7. Aligning the Unit

The final step in developing unit foundations for instruction is unit alignment. Once you have created the unit foundations, you need to use them as a guide for designing the individual lessons, objectives, assessment, subject area standards, and the national, state, and local standards. This is called unit alignment.

Think of it this way: A unit is composed of many parts that need to be meaningfully related. The key focus for a unit is that all instruction should, in some way, be directed toward students' understanding of the enduring idea for the unit. Unit objectives, lesson objectives, instructional activities, and assessment criteria and tasks must be aligned. In addition, the important ideas and skills addressed in the unit need to be consistent with subject area (discipline) standards, and other appropriate local, state, and/or national standards. Checking these relationships can be an effective way of assessing unit construction during or after completing a unit design.

Choosing Enduring Ideas

Earlier in the chapter, we listed and provided examples of enduring ideas such as identity, justice, relationships, interdependence, survival, power, humans and nature, conflict, celebration, freedom, emotions, and spirituality. However, we do not proscribe any single list of enduring ideas that should be included in the art curriculum. This will depend upon judgments made at the local level about the relevance of the enduring idea in regard to specific student populations, art understandings, meaningfulness beyond the classroom, connections to contemporary culture, and prospects for future significance in students' lives.

The safety net, so to speak, is the definition of enduring ideas proposed earlier in this chapter. The qualifications for an enduring idea inherently cast learning in terms of significance.

Given that enduring ideas are broad, encompassing human concerns that occur over time, they are inherently applicable to multiple contexts. In fact, they demand being repeatedly taught through a range of topics, artworks, and cultural contexts if they are to be fully understood. The same enduring ideas can thus be included in the curriculum at various grade levels.

A frequent and troublesome mistake is selection for the curriculum of enduring ideas that are not broad enough to qualify as such. For example, families or peer groups might be topics that would fall under the enduring idea of relationships rather than qualifying as enduring ideas themselves. Families and peer groups have diverse possibilities for study, but the idea of relationships, a more abstract notion, is even broader. Remember, the selection of enduring ideas for the curriculum should be guided by how important the idea is for students, what important connections the idea has with art, and what its significance for contemporary culture is.

Long after students have encountered a study of contemporary artworks, they will probably have forgotten many of the details about artworks, titles, dates, artists' names, media, styles, and techniques; but they may well remember the power of artworks to question the society we live in or raise awareness of the complexities of human relationships. Which is more regrettable—to forget titles, dates, names, influences, artistic styles, and locations or to miss understanding that artworks play a significant role in revealing the world around us? In proposing a plan for curriculum work, we propose an emphasis on significant content and active student inquiry. Enduring ideas serve this goal in directing curriculum content toward significance that provides compelling reasons for pursuing inquiry through art.

Notes

1 For clarity, we refer only to enduring ideas but recognize that the same concept may be exercised under other terminology such as themes, issues, or key ideas.

2 The Ohio State Faculty, "Integrated Curriculum: Possibilities for the Arts," *The Journal of Art Education* 55, no. 3 (May 2002), 12–22.

3 The TETAC curriculum units about identity were developed by Ms. Jossette Kluk at Columbus High School, Columbus, Nebraska, and Ms. Janet Parker at Woodland High School, Woodland, California, 2000.

4 E. D. Hirsch Jr., "Seeking Breadth and Depth in the Curriculum," *Educational Leadership* (October, 2001), 22–25.

5 The TETAC curriculum unit was created by Ms. Gloria Doering at Newton D. Baker Elementary School for the Arts in Cleveland, Ohio, 2000.

6 The TETAC curriculum unit was created by Ms. Sherri Pittard at Newton D. Baker Elementary School for the Arts in Cleveland, Ohio, 2000.

7 J. Stern, TETAC Mentor at Westbridge Middle School, 2001.

8 S. R. Walker and M. Parson, "School Reform and the Arts: Commentary," *Arts Policy and Review* (2000).

9 B. Rogers, "Informing the Shape of the Curriculum: New Views of Knowledge and Its Representation in Schooling," *Journal of Curriculum Studies* 29, no. 6 (1997), 686.

10 H. H. Jacobs, *Mapping the Big Picture: Integrating Curriculum and Assessment, K–12*, Alexandria, Va.: Association for Supervision and Curriculum Development, 1997.

11 R. Tyler, "Tyler's Rationale Reconsidered." In George Willis et al., eds., *The American Curriculum: A Documentary History* (Westport, Conn.: Greenwood Press, 1997), pp. 393–400.

12 L. Rongisch, "Reflecting on My Curriculum Unit." Unpublished manuscript. Tara Heights Elementary School, Papillon, Nebraska.

Chapter

4

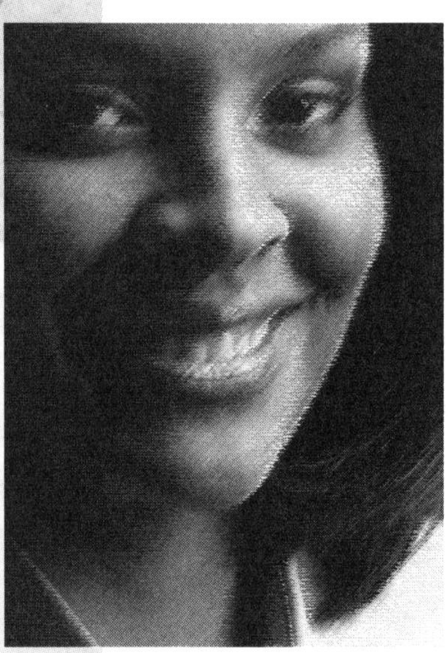

Making Choices: Selecting Lesson Content to Build on Unit Foundations

A curriculum should not be obsessed with comprehensiveness or fundamental skills. A lesson of living in a postmodern society of many cultures is that there are as many starting points as ending points in creating thoughtful, competent, aesthetically sophisticated people.

—Art educator Olivia Gude[1]

A Texas art teacher, second-grade teacher, and kindergarten teacher are planning a curriculum unit around the theme of human diversity and have chosen to study American postage stamps, an unusual choice for an art unit. How might the art teacher determine if a study of postage stamps would be appropriate content for the art curriculum? In another school setting, two high school art teachers from California are planning a curriculum unit with the installations of contemporary artist Sandy Skoglund. How might these art teachers determine if these fantasy installations are appropriate content for their art curriculum?

Although specific decisions about which artworks and artists to include in the curriculum are important, they are not the most basic considerations for selecting art content for the curriculum. In this chapter, we consider how to best develop students' understanding of art. We know from educational research that students often fail to retain much of the detail that informs learning. For this reason, we suggest that educators need to focus on the big picture—the larger issues, ideas, and inquiry processes that form knowledge— while *also* addressing specific art content. Because we believe that choices about artists, artworks, artifacts, and cultures must be made within a larger conceptual framework, this chapter will entertain questions about selecting artists, artworks, artifacts, and cultures for study only after pursuing a careful examination of specific inquiry processes related to the practices of responding to, making, and theorizing about art.

Art Knowledge: Ways of Knowing

In the 1960s at a crucial juncture in the history of art education curriculum, Manual Barkan contended that art criticism, art history, and artmaking should be at the core of art education curriculum. He simultaneously acknowledged that the arts are not formally structured bodies of knowledge. However, he observed:

[T]here are controls operating in competent work by artists, critics, and others engaged in art, and, to this important extent, they engage in structured inquiry which is disciplined. To this extent, too, inquiry into art curriculum can be both structured and disciplined and so can the curriculum itself.[2]

Unlike science education, which presents a structured body of knowledge in a consistent way, art education is not consistent in the way it presents con-

cepts, and varies from school to school and classroom to classroom. More recently, Arthur Efland has taken note of the ill-structured nature of art knowledge.[3] To Efland, art curriculum is a lattice-like structure that permits an overlapping of knowledge and concepts from the four art disciplines.[4] Instead of designing a hierarchy of knowledge that moves through the curriculum in a sequenced manner, concepts that guide the practice of artists, art critics, art historians, and aestheticians are revisited with a range of diverse artworks. Revisiting concepts with diverse examples advances student understanding of the complexity, contradictions, and ambiguities of the concepts.

To study art on a case-by-case basis with any success, however, students require a conceptual framework to provide the required connections between cases and to guide continuous art learning. Educational theorist Richard Prawat reminds us that "the expert's knowledge base is organized around a more central set of understandings or 'big ideas' than the novice's."[5] Prawat points to the example of the Wu Li dance master who advocates beginning any exercise from the center, not the fringe, and imparts the basic principles of the art prior to espousing the more meticulous details.[6] In a similar vein, we suggest a conceptual framework composed of key art understandings and inquiry concepts and principles from the four core areas previously identified as the locus of discipline-based art education: criticism, history, artmaking, and aesthetics.

Key Art Understandings

The identification of key art understandings to guide curriculum and instruction mirrors Prawat's notions of a curriculum matrix of big ideas, which he argues "represents a marked departure from the fixed agenda concept."[7] He suggests "setting two or three broad, general goals; once these have been specified,

Puzzling Lists

Art educator Olivia Gude was surprised at the disjunction between two lists she received from prospective art teachers in an art foundations class. In the first list, students were to enumerate areas in the visual arts that they found exciting and related to vital issues of contemporary culture and living. In the second list, students were to cite topics and issues for a curriculum for a beginning art class at the high school level. The differences in the two lists are worth contemplating.

Gude remarks that the first list contains many important ideas in making and valuing contemporary art, while the second consists mostly of study topics that could have been chosen for a beginning art class seventy-five or more years ago. Why did the students have such a difficult time imagining a more contemporary approach to art education? She concludes, "These emerging teachers, like many teachers currently in the field, are imaging their curriculum in the style, content, and methods of their earlier education, rather than reflecting the reality of

List One	List Two
Exciting Areas in the Visual Arts	**Topics for a Beginning Art Class**
• Legitimacy of artmaking with appropriated images from popular culture	• Elements and principles of design
• Controversial artworks in the news	• Printmaking
• Feminist art that utilizes media traditionally associated with women	• Color mixing
	• Painting
• The possibility of finding universal values in art	• Figure drawing
	• Making art on the computer
• Architecture	• Impressionism
	• Surrealism
• Collaborative community art	• Pop art

contemporary art and their own understandings of contemporary culture.

Source: "Investigating the Culture of Curriculum." In Dennis E. Fehr, Kris Fehr, and Karen Keifer-Boyd (eds.), *Real-World Readings in Art Education: Things Your Professor Never Told You* (New York: Palmer Press, 2000).

Wilson's List: Things That Art Teachers of the 21st Century Should Possess, Know, Understand, and Be Able to Do Well

Following are some of the items on art educator Brent Wilson's list.

The art teacher in the twenty-first century should possess:

- a knowledge of a canon of important artworks that center art instruction. Canon refers not to a master list of works, but rather is loose and changing including masterworks as well as works of local significance, minor works, and contemporary and traditional works.

- a knowledge of the ideas in this canon of works and the ways they relate to the history of ideas.

- a knowledge of the conditions that surround the works in this canon.

- a knowledge of the ways in which art historians, sociologists of art, and art critics have interpreted the works in this canon.

The art teacher in the twenty-first century should be able to:

- guide students of different ages and developmental levels to interpret the meanings of the works in this canon for themselves through the act of criticism.

- guide students with reinterpreting the meanings of the works in this canon through the processes of artistic creation.

- guide students in studying the social, cultural, historical, and individual conditions that surround the creation of this canon of artworks.

Source: "Postmodernism and the Challenge of Content: Teaching Teachers of Art for the Twenty-first Century." In N. C. Yakel (ed.), *The Future: Challenge of Change* (Reston, VA: National Art Education Association, 1992).

Looking Back

In 1899 Arthur Wesley Dow introduced an art curriculum based upon the elements and principles of design. By the 1930s this idea, grounded in a formalist belief system, began to appear in art curriculum guides.

Looking Forward

"What are they teaching art students these days?" This query framed Gail Gregg's investigation of how art is taught at the university level. In an article chronicling this search, this author and artist remarks, "the last half-century has seen a revolution in the way art is taught in this country." What has changed? One difference, Gregg notes, is that today artists need to have so much more cultural knowledge and relate their work to the contemporary world and the historical canon. Another surprising fact she cites is that many schools over the past decade have dropped art history as a requirement and replaced it with courses in cultural theory or history or anthropology. She also quotes Carol Becker, vice president for academic affairs at the Art Institute of Chicago, who says "faculties spend more time today helping students explain their work and place it in a contemporary context."

Source: G. Gregg, "What Are They Teaching Art Students These Days?" *Art News* 102, no. 4 (April 2003), pp. 106–109.

one can engage in a sort of conceptual analysis that yields a series of big ideas relevant to each major goal."[8] Importantly, Prawat stresses that one should be mindful not only of the ideas but of the relationships among the ideas as well. The following list of key art understandings is drawn directly from the final project report of the Transforming Education Through the Arts Challenge (TETAC).

- Art is a purposeful human endeavor.
- Art attains value, purpose, and meaning from the personal, social, and cultural dimensions of life.
- Art raises philosophical issues and questions.
- Artworks are objects for interpretation.
- Change is fundamental to art.

These five understandings contain the seeds of much that is central to art, embodying a complexity that will not be learned in a single encounter, course, grade level, or even a single individual's education from kindergarten through college. These ideas necessitate repeated instruction in multiple contexts, represent a host or network of related understandings, and often generate new inquiry. Put simply, they represent issues requiring lifelong learning.

An effective way to focus on key art understandings is to ask, What do I want my students to retain and understand about art long after they have left my classroom? This overriding objective is best achieved through an inquiry approach derived from the four key areas of art study.

Art Criticism: A Conceptual Framework

Just what should students understand about art criticism? In brief, students should understand that criticism is primarily about interpreting the meanings of artworks and evaluating their qualities. Art critics ask key questions such as What do you see? What is the artwork about? What tells you that? Is it good art?[9]

The modes of inquiry for art criticism derive from practices of description, analysis, interpretation, and judgment.

In general, the art criticism principles organized around these practices are most related to the key art understandings that "artworks are objects for interpretation" and that "art attains value, purpose, and meaning from the personal, social, and cultural dimensions of life." That is, as students interpret and judge different artworks, they should become aware that art has "aboutness" and that the interpretive meaning and evaluation of artworks derives from a range of sources. As students engage in describing, analyzing, interpreting, and judging artworks, they also need to stretch their understandings. The goal is to shape and deepen the students' understandings of the processes that inform areas of art practice.

Art Criticism in Practice: Humans, Memorials, and Suffering

To deepen their understanding that artworks have aboutness and that this aboutness deals with significant human issues and events, a class of California high school students engaged in a critical exercise involving sculptor Kenneth Treister's *Holocaust Memorial* (1990), a monumental sculpture commissioned by Holocaust survivors living in Miami, Florida, to commemorate the deaths of six million Jews under the Nazi regime.[10] The enduring idea for the unit, human suffering, shaped the art criticism discussions as students sketched views of Treister's memorial, described the sculpture, and interpreted its meaning. They also watched *Playing for Time*, a video about the women of the Holocaust who, in order to spare their lives, formed an orchestra to play for the Nazi officers. The video and class discussions broadened their knowledge about the historical period and hence deepened their interpretations of Treister's memorial.

FAQs

What is the best way to learn a subject?

"The best way to learn a subject is to learn its general principles and to study an ample number of diverse examples that illustrate those principles."

—E. D. Hirsch Jr.

"There is a limit to how much understanding of a complex entity can be achieved in a single treatment in a single context, for a single purpose. By repeating the presentation of the same complex case or concept information in *new contexts,* the multi-facetedness of these 'landscape sites' are brought out. . . ."

—R. J. Spiro et al.

Sources: E. D. Hirsch Jr., "Seeking Breadth and Depth in the Curriculum," *Educational Leadership,* October 2001, p. 23. R. Spiro et al., cited in Arthur Efland, "The Spiral and the Lattice: Changes in Cognitive Learning Theory with Implications for Art Education," *Studies in Art Education* 36, no. 3 (1995), p. 145.

4.1 Kenneth Treister, Holocaust Memorial, *Central Sculpture and Lily Pool, Miami Beach, 2.5 acre garden, reflection pool and arbor surrounding a 50-foot-high cast bronze sculpture depicting the victims of the Holocaust clinging precariously to an outstretched arm.*

Art Criticism Principles

Describing Art

- Descriptions account for subject matter, medium, form, and context.

- Description can be intrinsic or extrinsic.

- Descriptive language is never value-free.

- Good descriptions use rich, robust, revealing language.

- Descriptions, like interpretations, are meaningfully circular.

Interpreting Art

- Artworks are always about something.

- Feelings are guides to interpretations.

- Interpretations are intended to persuade.

- Interpretation does not have to match the artist's intent.

- All art is in part about the world from which it emerged.

- An artwork can have more than one interpretation.

- Some interpretations are better than others.

- Interpretations are not right or wrong but convincing and informative.

- Good interpretations have coherence, correspondence, and inclusiveness.

- Good interpretations tell more about the artwork than they do about the interpreter.

- Artworks are meant to be interpreted metaphorically and not literally.

- Interpretations are about artworks, not artists.

- Any artwork will allow a range of interpretations.

- Successful interpretations are more or less reasonable, convincing, informative, and enlightening.

Judging Art

- Judgments are different from preferences.

- Judgments about artworks should be supported with evidence.

- Communal consensus strengthens the validity of judgments.

- Judgments should be well reasoned.

- Judgments, like interpretations, should be persuasive arguments.

- There are multiple criteria for judging works of art.

- Some judgments should be taken more seriously than others.

- Judgments should tell more about the artwork than the person judging.

- Artworks, not artists, are the objects of judgments.

Source: Terry Barrett, *Interpreting Art, Criticizing Art: Understanding the Contemporary.* 2nd ed. (Mountain View, CA: Mayfield Publishers, 2000).

As a conclusion to their critique, students were asked to explain the evidence for their interpretation. To do so required students to consider the merits of different kinds of evidence for interpretation. That is, the visual qualities of the memorial sculpture might not be the only means of interpretation. Contextual evidence outside the artwork such as historical information, other memorial sculptures, and critical commentary might also become evidence for interpretation. Students had to not only cite evidence but also weigh and assess it.

The following student response to the art criticism exercise was accompanied by a sketch of Treister's forty-two-foot-high bronze sculpture of an overscaled arm and hand, rising skyward from the earth, and layered with numerous small human figures silently crying out in desperate anguish.

The hand is reaching upward toward God from the ground, the resting place of the dead. The hand symbolizes the voices of Holocaust dead, as a whole, appealing to God and all those who stood by and watched the suffering. The hand could also symbolize the image of the Jews as the heroic survivors, from the persecuted population to the survivors of Hitler's regime to the founders of Israel.

This student's interpretation amply demonstrates the art criticism principle that all art is in part about the world from which it has emerged, a particularly appropriate interpretive strategy for Treister's memorial. Seeking significant and relevant connections to the larger world can deepen interpretation and remind students that artworks are produced and exist within a social context.

Cognitive research recognizes the close association between knowledge and problem solving.[11] Creativity research identifies breadth of knowledge as a key personality trait among creative thinkers.[12] It is imperative to bring both general and artistic knowledge to art instruction. Imagine the thinness of the California high school students' interpretations of Treister's memorial sculpture if they had little knowledge of the Holocaust.

Art Criticism and Aesthetic Issues

To conclude the curriculum unit on the *Holocaust Memorial*, the high school art teachers led a class discussion about society's moral obligation to respond to persecution and the artist's ethical responsibility to create works that reflect such persecution. The nature of the commissioned *Holocaust Memorial* readily lent itself to philosophical questions about the social purposes of artworks and the social role of artists. As we describe later in the chapter, philosophical questions often emerge from art criticism. This discussion was also an opportunity to link the instruction to the unit's enduring idea of human suffering and to extend the instruction beyond the study of a single artwork to contemplate a broad art understanding with implications for many artworks and artists.

Art History: A Conceptual Framework

Study of the history of art is about time, chronology, classification, material objects that have been designated as artworks, aesthetics, style, intellectual ideas, interpretation, analysis, evaluation, iconography, social and cultural context, and change. Art historians ask key questions such as What accounts for an artwork's artistic character? Why do artworks change over time? and Where do artworks belong in the larger art-historical scheme?

The practices of art criticism and art history are similar—art critics are concerned with art of the present while art historians deal with art of the past. Both

Practicing Criticism

What do critics do?

Arthur Efland observes that critics do not
rely upon formal principles or universal
standards as a source of methods for
approaching the work but rely instead
upon their individualized personal history
of cases built through individual encounters with artworks. "Their knowledge is a
'knowledge in practice rather than in the
abstract.'"

Source: A. Efland, "The Spiral and the Lattice: Changes in Cognitive Learning Theory
with Implications for Art Education," *Studies in Art Education* 36, no. 3 (1995), p. 146.

are concerned with interpreting and evaluating artworks. Art historians are occupied with placing artworks within the context of other artworks and art
movements. They care about how and why art
changes. Art critics deal with this question by examining how contemporary artists push the boundaries
and nature of art.

Unlike art critics, art historians deal with questions
about who made a given artwork and where the artwork originated. These inquiries by art historians can
help students understand art through the lens of the
past and raise the questions of why art changes and
why it is the way it is.

Art History in Practice: A Sense of Place

Students in grades 4 and 5 in a school in New Orleans
became art historians as they used the enduring idea
of the sense of place to study works by painter Will
Henry Stevens. The curriculum unit, "Will Henry
Stevens and a Place for Me," challenged students with
a key art-historical question: Why are the works of
this artist the way they are?[13]

As a painter, Stevens created a large body of work
during the midtwentieth century, at times experi-
menting with modernist abstraction and nonobjective
forms but always continuing to work directly from
nature.[14] Quite interested in the natural world, he
explored and painted the waterways of the Mississippi River and Gulf Coast around New Orleans and
other parts of Louisiana, and the mountain ranges in
the Southern Highlands of North Carolina.

Beginning with an Enduring Idea

In the introductory lesson, the students focused on
the enduring idea of place, considering the essential
question "What makes a place unique?" They listed
numerous things that were part of their own city of

Art-Historical Concepts and Principles

Description

- Artworks can be identified by artist, date, place of origin, materials, techniques, physical condition, patronage, and authenticity.

- Direct and indirect evidence can be used in identifying artworks.

- Artworks can be classified according to style, iconography (subject matter and themes) and time period.

Analysis

- Formal analysis is about style, materials, and techniques.

- Extrinsic analysis is about purpose and function.

- Artworks from the same or different time period or place can be compared and contrasted.

Interpretation

- Artworks are shaped by location, time period, and cultural context.

- Artworks are shaped by social, political, and economic factors.

- Artworks are shaped by artistic, philosophical, religious, and intellectual ideas.

- Artworks can be explained in terms of the artist's biography.

- Artworks can be explained in terms of iconography, i.e., the artwork's subject matter and themes.

- Artworks can be explained in terms of standard conventions and symbols.

- Style can be related to the characteristics of the culture which produced it.

- Change in art can be explained in terms of physical, social, cultural, and technological factors.

- Artworks feature certain ideas, values, and attitudes while marginalizing or ignoring others.

- Artworks are shaped by multiple factors.

Evaluation

- Artworks can be placed in a hierarchical order.

- Criteria for evaluating artworks changes over time.

Source: These art history concepts and principles derive primarily from the work of art historian Martin Rosenberg. See M. Rosenberg, "Concepts from Dialogue of Participants in the DBAE Symposium," Joslyn Art Museum, January 21 and February 25, 1989.

New Orleans, such as streetcars, steamboats and barges, Mardi Gras, jazz, and the Mississippi River.

In another activity for the unit, the students generated a list of Japanese design elements such as asymmetry, cropping, strong diagonal lines, and multiple viewpoints. While this activity and the previous list they generated about New Orleans appear totally unrelated, both were linked to the work of Will Henry Stevens. His richly hued pastels and paintings combine the uniqueness of specific American locales such as New Orleans with design qualities derived from Japanese woodblock prints. When the fourth and fifth graders visited the Ogden Museum of Southern Art, they were able to identify both of these characteristic qualities in Stevens's paintings and pastels. Further, in comparing color differences and horizon lines in Stevens's pastel drawings from New Orleans and North Carolina, the students grasped the artist's intent to express the distinctive physical qualities of each locale. Students were beginning to understand why artworks look the way they do. However, to fully comprehend the concept, they needed further information.

Engaging in Art-Historical Inquiry

To help students explore the question of why Stevens's artworks look the way they do, the teachers, Nancy Lilly and Ann Rowson Love, presented the fourth graders with an extraordinary cache of contextual information that included family archival materials and writings by art historian Jessie Poesch and Will Henry Stevens himself. Students also had the unusual opportunity to interview a former student of Stevens, Louise Keppler, who had studied with him in the early 1940s at Sophie Newcomb College in New Orleans. As they interviewed Ms. Keppler, the fourth and fifth graders discovered more about the artist's working

methods and Stevens's outdoor sketching trips. They learned how he drew pastels directly from nature, produced intricate color maps that recreated a color palette of the site, and later used them to complete the artworks in the studio.

The students also learned of Stevens's encounter with Chinese landscape painting at the Freer Gallery of Art in Washington and the influence of Taoism and Eastern philosophies on his art. With this information, students began to make connections between his work and the Japanese design elements. The two lists that the fourth and fifth graders had created in the introductory lesson no longer seemed so incongruous.

Will Henry Stevens once said, "For my part I must feel rooted to a place, a sort of ownership in it, or I cannot take the expression of it seriously."[15] The New Orleans students further discovered that although Stevens lived away from the established art centers of New York and the East Coast, he had studied at the Art Students League in New York, knew members of the Ash Can School, and during his life continued to travel regularly in order to remain informed about leading artistic developments. His encounters with the art and theories of Wassily Kandinsky and Paul Klee redirected his work toward abstraction and the organic biomorphic forms of nature. Yet he also continued to work in a more representational form as well. In the late 1930s, Stevens wrote, "I do not draw a line between objective and nonobjective and have painted in the former way this winter and will continue to do so when I feel I have something to say in this way."[16]

Armed with all this information, the students constructed their own meanings about why Stevens's works look the way they do. Their learning went beyond simply accumulating so many facts about the

4.2 *Fourth/fifth grade students and TETAC mentor Ann Rowson Love at the Ogden Museum of Southern Art, New Orleans, viewing the work of painter Will Henry Stevens.*

4.3 *Will Henry Stevens, Untitled, pastel, 15 3/4" x 21", 1938*

4.4 *Will Henry Stevens, Untitled, gouache, 20" x 16", 1941*

Practicing Art History

What do art historians do?

Art historian Alois Reigl explains his work as,
". . . some of us are convinced that the mission of
our discipline is not simply to find the things of the
past that appeal to modern taste, but to delve into
the artistic volition (*Kuntswollen*) behind works of
art and to discover why they are they way they are,
and why they could not have been otherwise."

Reigl's inquiry—why are artworks the way they are—
is the same question that guided the New Orleans
fourth graders in their study of Will Henry Stevens
described beginning on page 46.

Source: A. Reigl, "Preface." In *The Group Portraiture of
Holland.* Introduction by Wolfgang Kemp; translations
by Evelyn M. Kain and David Britt (Los Angeles: Getty
Research Center for the History of Art and the Humanities, 1999). Originally published as an article in 1902.

4.5 *Students need to be encouraged to take seriously
their role as art makers. They should be helped to see
that they have both a history of artmaking and a
future; that the process of making is ongoing.*

artist and his artworks. The fourth and fifth graders
practiced art history in an experiential manner.

By designing art-historical learning from a perspective of inquiry, teachers can show students how to
deal with information about an artist in a more
meaningful manner. In the curriculum unit based on
Stevens, students learned that artworks are shaped by
artistic, philosophical, religious, and intellectual ideas;
artworks can be explained in terms of an artist's biography; and, most important for Stevens's work, artworks are shaped by location, time period, and
cultural context. Given these concepts and principles,
the fourth and fifth graders could make meaningful
connections between the information they possessed
about Stevens and his artworks. Without these concepts and principles to guide them, it would have
been more difficult to construct these connections
and to consider questions such as Was the artist's lay-
ering technique influenced by other artists and art
movements? Was it about expressing the uniqueness
of a specific place? and Was it about the nonobjective
art theories he had encountered?

The two teachers spent much time preparing this
curriculum unit. The students' experience with
Stevens's work was exceptional—they viewed original artworks, investigated a local artist who reflects
the local geography, and interviewed a student who
had studied with the artist. Realistically, not every
curriculum unit can be developed to this extent.
However, this unit suggests that the deeper the exploration, the better the results, and that a smaller
number of in-depth curriculum units may be more
effective than a great number of less well-conceived
learning experiences.

Artmaking: A Conceptual Framework

Artmaking is primarily taught to further technical skill,
design knowledge, and personal expression. We be-

Practicing Art History

What do art historians do?

How do art historians authenticate artworks of questionable authorship? The Rembrandt Research Project (RRP) conducted over the past thirty-five years, and still unfinished, has been heavily criticized for dropping too many of what had been considered genuine works. Thus far, the RRP has validated about three hundred Rembrandt pictures, half the number considered to be works by the Baroque master a century ago. Some of the methods used by the RRP to validate or invalidate the Rembrandt works are

- visual observations of the surfaces of the painting
- chemical analysis of paints and grounds for paintings
- thread counting of canvases (millions of threads were counted)
- dendrochronology—the study of tree rings—to date Rembrandt's wood panel paintings
- x-ray to look at how brushstrokes were formulated and layers of paint applied over others
- biographical information about where the artist was located in certain time periods, and
- inquiries into practices of collecting at the beginning of the eighteenth century.

Dutch scholar Ernst van de Wetering, one of the two principal RRP committee members along with Dutch scholar Joshua Bruyn, describes his way of looking at Rembrandts as influenced by his background as a painter. He remarks, "I never looked at them as images but as processes. Bruyn isn't a painter. He has an incredible memory and a very good eye, but it's a different eye from mine—and why not?" As a result of his highly controversial experience with the RRP, Bruyn eventually resigned from the committee. Van de Wetering concludes that "connoisseurship by committee does not bring a greater truth. We know too little, so what does consensus say in front of the vast hole in which we only see scattered fragments of the past?"

Source: S. Hochfield, "What Is a Real Rembrandt?" *Art News* 103, no. 2 (February 2004), pp. 82–93.

lieve that artmaking is also a means for exploring the world, self, and others. In his acclaimed analysis of Picasso's *Guernica,* psychologist Rudolf Arnheim remarks that "Picasso did not simply deposit in *Guernica* what he had thought about the world; rather did he further his understanding of the world through the making of *Guernica*."[17] Contemporary painter Brice Marden has remarked, "I think that painting, or the kind of painting I prefer to explore, is about unknowns or looking for questions more than for answers."[18] These remarks from Arnheim and Marden mirror our approach to classroom artmaking and the concepts and principles that we identify for artmaking practice.[19]

The artmaking principles outlined in the sidebar on page 53 are well-known and characteristic ways of making and instructing art. For instance, setting the conditions for artmaking is a commonplace and necessary practice for every artmaking experience, referring to decisions about media, subject matter, formal qualities, style, technique, scale, and context.*

In the following example, we demonstrate that it was the preparatory instruction from art criticism and art history that readied the students to engage artmaking as an inquiry process. We further stress that it

*For more on the artmaking process and related inquiry concepts and principles, see *Teaching Meaning in Artmaking,* a text in this same Art Education in Practice series.

was the purposeful inquiry shaping this project that engaged students in artmaking as a means of exploring the world and their place in it.

Artmaking in Practice: Bizarre Realities

As part of an art activity assignment, a group of California high school art students explored their school campus searching for outdoor scenes to capture with their digital cameras. After making digital photographs of everyday campus life, the students used Adobe Photoshop software to insert angels and demons, peering eyes, robotic figures, exploding office equipment, looming rainbows, skeletons, swimming fish, and levitated figures among the campus buildings, playing fields, outdoor seating areas, walkways, and student groups shown in the images.[20]

On the surface, this artmaking project might seem to be just an entertaining activity with little learning value. Employing technological media facilitated the students' manipulation of and experimentation with the digitized photographs, but what was the activity about? What ideas, conceptual possibilities, or artmaking problem focused the project? Was the objective simply to create bizarre situations by inserting curious elements into everyday campus scenes?

Artist Sandy Skoglund, whose fantasy installations the California high school students studied in preparation for this artmaking project, has commented that she often engages in play, but it is "purposeful play." Skoglund presents everyday situations such as tenement kitchens, suburban living rooms, patios, low-rent offices, and urban bistros, depicted in highly unusual presentations. The tenement kitchen in Skoglund's *Radioactive Cats*, for instance, teems with clusters of prowling lime green cats, and the urban bistro in *Fox Games* is enlivened by a pack of crimson red foxes leaping over restaurant tables and chairs. In studying Skoglund's fantastic worlds, the high school

art students investigated the unit's enduring idea of social reality. Students found that combining the normal and abnormal can raise doubts about what is often taken for granted. For instance, Skoglund's suburban patio scene depicted in *Gathering Paradise*, populated with more than a hundred squirrels, is abnormal enough to raise questions as to the boundaries between humans and nature in this artificial suburban environment. Discussing the Skoglund installations, the high school students asked, What are social norms? How are they constructed? How do they affect our behavior?

In a writing assignment, prior to creating their altered digitized photographs, the students were instructed to describe a familiar everyday scene and to convey the scene in increasingly strange terms with each succeeding paragraph. After reading their compositions to the entire class, the high school students discussed social norms, what society considers normal, and hidden fears that may exist in ordinary environments.

When students finally began to disrupt their digital photographs with strangeness, they were considering issues of reality, society, and social norms that had begun to take shape in their discussions of Skoglund's fantasized worlds. Their task was to further explore this problem in the context of their school campus.

As this artmaking experience demonstrates, it was instructionally important that it be carefully conceived and planned. Prior to the artmaking, the art teachers held a review session to discuss

- the degree of separation between the normal and the bizarre,
- how situations may appear normal to some, but abnormal to others, and
- how standards of normalcy are culturally derived.

Artmaking Concepts and Principles

Building a Knowledge Base

- Knowledge of other artists' artworks is essential for artmaking.

- Knowledge from diverse nonartistic sources can usefully inform artmaking.

- A well-funded knowledge base is fundamental for substantive artmaking.

- Conducting formal and informal research is a con-sequential aspect of artmaking practice.

Finding Personal Connections

- Artmaking requires personal investment if it is to become more than an exercise.

- Personal connections derive from multiple sources.

- Personal connections can be extended beyond the personal to larger social meanings.

Problem Finding and Solving

- Predetermining a big idea, issue, or theme for art-making focuses problem finding.

- Artmaking problems are often initially ill-defined.

- Artmaking problems can change during the art-making process.

- Delay in closure can produce more innovative and less predictable ideas.

- Conceptual strategies can generate new perspectives.

Setting Conditions for Artmaking

- Boundaries for artmaking can motivate innovation and creativity.

- Boundaries for artmaking should be meaningful.

Finding the Visual Form

- The visual form of the artwork embodies metaphorical meaning.

- The visual form of the artwork is often initially ill-defined.

- The visual form of the artwork evolves over time.

- Change to visual form is a vital part of the art-making process.

- Manipulating media, formal qualities, and imagery can create new conceptual possibilities.

- Experimentation with the non-conventional can stimulate new ideas.

- Purposeful play can create new conceptual possibilities.

- Pushing boundaries with media can create new conceptual possibilities.

Source: The above principles derive from the work of Sydney Walker. See *Teaching Meaning in Artmaking* (Worcester, MA: Davis Publications, 2001).

Because the high school students had already begun to think about social reality in their class discussions, writing assignments, and interpretations of Skoglund's installations, their manipulations and experiments to alter the normality of their school environment were directed toward meaning, not simply strangeness and oddness. Their work reflected the spirit of the artmaking principles, which maintain that manipulation and experimentation are *purposeful* activities to create new conceptual possibilities. The computer technology permitted students to critically evaluate their decisions as they worked, rethinking ideas, making changes, and assessing the results until they found satisfactory solutions.

The familiarity of artmaking instruction often blinds us to what is important for students to learn from making art. Students may be actively engaged, but what are they learning? We might return to Dewey's comments, cited in Chapter 3, about not mistaking activity and student involvement for authentic learning. This represents a persistent problem with classroom artmaking. Often, guidance is limited to technical skills and design elements and principles. Structures or strategies for exploring ideas are usually nonexistent. Yet if students are to engage in the exploration of ideas through artmaking, the curriculum unit must concretely address inquiry principles and exploration of ideas that are directly linked to the artmaking experience.

Aesthetics: A Conceptual Framework

Aesthetics addresses the big questions about art that have intrigued and puzzled philosophers and ordinary people over time. These are questions related to beliefs about the purpose, value, meaning, and nature of art. Marilyn Stewart contends that "there is much to be gained by spending some time exploring our own views and those of others about art."[21]

These issues have traditionally been approached through philosophical questioning, philosophical dialogue, and aesthetic theory. It is important for teachers to design curriculum units that lead students to engage in philosophical discussions and questions about art as they explore art in the context of art criticism, art history, and artmaking. This necessitates that teachers possess a keen understanding of the nature of philosophical questions and dialogue about art. In the following classroom example, we demonstrate the principle that it is attention to the *general* that characterizes philosophical content. The curriculum unit's conceptual purpose is clearly connected to philosophical issues. That is, the nature of public art and monumental sculpture readily suggests philosophical questions about the purposes of art, concept, and valuing of art.

Aesthetics in Practice: Monuments

Nebraska elementary art teacher Deborah Kippley composed the following narrative for a sixth-grade curriculum unit, a study of public monuments located in and outside of the local Nebraska community. She wrote:

Since the beginning of recorded human history, human beings have left their mark on the geographic sites they reside in. It happened in France where early individuals drew images deep inside their caves in Lascaux. It happened in England as people hauled twenty-eight-ton rocks to a site on the Salisbury plain to create what we call Stonehenge. It happened across America as groups created mounds that could only be fully appreciated from an altitude that the creators could not achieve. It happened in Egypt and in Mexico where people built great towers to their gods. It happens today with artists like Claus Oldenburg and Coosje Van Brugggen who have created

Teacher Talk

The following comments from art teachers came at the conclusion of a university art course about the artmaking process based on the practices and principles found in the sidebar "Artmaking Concepts and Principles" (page 53).

- Kerrie King, an Ohio high school art teacher:

  "My philosophy throughout my undergraduate years and as an art educator has always been to familiarize myself with as much artistic media as possible so I could provide my students with a wide variety of media choices. . . . However, from this class, I began to question my role as an artist and as an art instructor. Should art educators be providing vast amounts of instruction about media and techniques or should they concentrate on teaching how an artist thinks as he or she uses this media? That was when I realized this class would have a strong impact on how I think about art and artmaking."

- Rachel Losch, a Tennessee elementary art teacher:

  "In the McCarthy and Sherlock article about teaching drawing, I struggled most with the idea that there should be no preconceptions as to the final outcome."

- Meredith Jones, an Ohio elementary art teacher:

  "Although I realize students need some guidelines, making cookie-cutter art projects is not my intent. I feel guidelines or boundaries are to help students think through a process and arrive at a solution to a question."

- Krista Albers, an Ohio middle school teacher:

  "Making art about an interesting design or learning a particular technique with a specific medium is a hard trap not to fall into."

- Teresa Roberts, a Tennessee high school teacher:

  "Art classes should not be a rehearsal for making 'real' art. Nor should they be technical workshops, where students learn skills and tools, which they may later use in a meaningful way. Students should be engaged in the same types of activities as real artists."

- Kate Menke, Ohio high school art teacher:

  "I was yearning for a technique or process that would provide a means of discovery and passion for my students. This class changed the way I think about art and the way I feel art should be taught. Before the class I could tell you that art was a language, but after the class I understood how I could use it as a language to communicate what I wanted to say about the world. . . . The world opened up for me and I realized my class could be a setting in which students were reflective about their world and their experiences."

- Andrew Moffatt, Ohio elementary art teacher:

  "I was intrigued by the idea that boundaries actually aid creative thinking, rather than impair it. I became rather obsessed with Chuck Close this quarter. He compared the problem-creating process to 'putting rocks in your shoes.' By chance I also heard Close in a radio interview in which he expressed how glad he was that he settled on boundaries (my word, not his) that added the structure to his work."

FAQs

How can I balance teaching skills and teaching for meaning?

This question frequently occurs as art teachers prepare to focus instruction on enduring ideas. We suggest thinking about the question What is it that I want my students to retain long after they have left my classroom? What could students, for instance, learn about the key art understandings, as posed in the introduction of this chapter, from participating in artmaking devoted to high levels of technical skill? Most probably, if artmaking is primarily focused on skill building, these key goals will be neither relevant nor achieved. On the other hand, if artmaking is completely devoid of skills and technique, meaning-making will be limited. This returns us to our initial question, how do we balance teaching skills and meaning? Art educator Olivia Gude writes, "I cringe when I see students spending weeks constructing and painting a color wheel and a value scale." She continues, "This is not to say that building skills for seeing, analyzing, and manipulating forms is no longer an important part of an art curriculum. However, we need to shift metaphors and recognize that these things are not foundational; they are not what are absolutely needed before contemporary issues of visual art and contemporary culture are needed."

Source: "Investigating the Culture of Curriculum." In Dennis E. Fehr, Kris Fehr, and Karen Keifer-Boyd (eds.), *Real-World Readings in Art Education: Things Your Professor Never Told You* (New York: Palmer Press, 2000).

monumental sculptures based on images from popular culture. From the time humans stepped foot on the earth, they have changed their environment for practical reasons, for aesthetic reasons, to establish ownership, and to celebrate their own existence or the existence of their creator.

In this unit, sixth-grade students examined a range of monuments and monumental sculpture within the context of the time, place, and culture of their creation. The subjects of their investigation were Stonehenge and a contemporary version of this English monument, *Carhenge* by Jim Reinders; Egyptian and Greek sculpture from the British Museum in London; and *Torn Notebook* by Oldenburg and Van Bruggen. Studying a range of diverse examples provided the sixth graders with an opportunity to engage in philosophical dialogue about the purposes of art, public monuments, and monumental sculpture. Focusing the unit upon several different examples of monumental sculpture more readily motivated this philosophical dialogue than perhaps would have been the case had the unit been about a single work.[22]

In addition to philosophical questions about the purposes of art, inquiry into how art acquires value would also be appropriate. For example, do we consider Stonehenge and the Egyptian and Greek sculptures more significant than *Torn Notebook* because they represent religious and spiritual connections? *Torn Notebook* challenges the serious nature of the usual subject matter associated with monumental sculpture. Or we might ask, is *Carhenge* less significant than Stonehenge? As a memorial to the artist's father, *Carhenge* is more personal in purpose. Why is *Carhenge* preserved and maintained by a special group, Friends of Carhenge? What value do they find in this work located on farmland near Alliance, Nebraska, that belonged to the artist's father? Is the monumental sculpture limited to local values or does *Carhenge* represent values found in other public sculptures?

These questions demonstrate how shifting class-room dialogue between the specific and the general can give rise to philosophical questions. The inquiry began with a general philosophical question about how art is valued, yielded to more specific concerns about single artworks, and then led to consideration of further general philosophical issues.

Further philosophical dialogue about art and value might emerge from considering whose values count when an artwork is of a public nature. How did the Greeks determine which sculptures were worthy of public display? Do we use the same standards today for public sculpture? Are there universal criteria for public sculpture? Why was *Torn Notebook* publicly critcized when it was installed on the grounds of the Sheldon Memorial Art Gallery in Lincoln, Nebraska? Did the monumental sculpture violate some universal criteria for public sculpture?

Philosophical questions regarding the concept of art are also embedded in this unit. It would be unusual if some of the sixth graders did not question whether a group of thirty-eight upright cars in a pas-ture is really art. The mysterious issues surrounding Stonehenge and its unknown origins and purposes raise further questions about its status as art and the concept of art itself.

The art teacher made wise curriculum choices for this unit. She selected a range of artworks that encouraged the investigation of philosophical con-cepts and questions. As suggested elsewhere here by Efland and others, art concepts attain complexity through examination of diverse works. Note, too, that two of the artworks, *Carhenge* and *Torn Notebook*, are found in the students' local Nebraska community,

FAQs

What is art?

Philosopher and art critic Arthur Danto argues that "an object is an artwork at all only in relation to an interpretation."

Source: A. Danto, *The Philosophical Disen-franchisement of Art* (New York: Columbia University Press, 1986), p. 44.

a factor that infused the philosophical issues with authenticity.

The inclusion of aesthetics in the curriculum raises art content to a level that exceeds specific artists, art-works, and contexts. If the sixth-grade curriculum unit had not compared different monuments to address the larger questions of how monuments are valued, student learning would have been considerably diminished. Studying philosophical questions and issues in the context of specific works is highly effec-tive but, as earlier recognized, demands the ability to recognize such opportunities.*

Interweaving Inquiry Processes for Key Understandings

Although we have presented a separate focus on key understandings of art, inquiry principles, art history, art criticism, artmaking, and aesthetics, we have illus-trated how these four art areas function independ-

*For more about teaching aesthetics, see M. Stewart, *Thinking Through Aesthetics,* a text in this same Art Education in Practice series.

Aesthetic Concepts and Principles

Philosophical Questioning

- Philosophical questions are open-ended, but defensible.
- Philosophical questions inquire about the concepts of art.
- Philosophical questions inquire about the purposes of art.
- Philosophical questions inquire about the meaning of art.
- Philosophical questions inquire about value of art.
- Philosophical questions inquire about the judgment of art.

Philosophical Dialogue

- Philosophical arguments are well reasoned.
- Philosophical arguments use careful language.
- Philosophical arguments employ well-chosen examples.
- Philosophical arguments use aesthetic theories for support.

Aesthetic Theory

- Philosophical theories account for how art acquires meaning.
- Philosophical theories account for the nature of art.
- Philosophical theories account for the nature of art-making.
- Philosophical theories account for the nature of artists.
- The philosophical practices and principles derive from the work of Marilyn Stewart.
- Philosophical theories account for the purposes of art.
- Philosophical theories account for how the art is judged.
- Philosophical theories account for how art acquires value.

Source: The above philosophical practices and principles derive from the work of Marilyn Stewart. See Marilyn G. Stewart, *Thinking Through Aesthetics* (Worcester, MA: Davis Publications, 1999).

ently. As was clear in the artmaking example based on Skoglund's work from the California high school, it was the knowledge from art criticism that informed the students' artmaking. In the art criticism example of students who studied the *Holocaust Memorial*, a major philosophical issue developed around the notion of human suffering and the implications for artwork and artists. Thus not only is art learning linked with the different areas of inquiry; by basing the art curriculum on the key art understandings, such understandings will function as the primary connectors for the art curriculum. They become the conceptual focus interweaving art inquiry from art criticism, art history, artmaking, and aesthetics. The California high school units, for example, one framed around human suffering and a historical event and the other around everyday life and human behavior, engaged students with the same key art understandings. That is, students may eventually forget the specific artworks studied in each unit or all their classmates' artworks, but it is highly likely that they began to develop a lasting comprehension that artworks are purposeful human endeavors and that they attain meaning from engaging with the personal and social dimensions of life. Further encounters with other artworks and artmaking could deepen and strengthen these key art understandings for the students.

In creating curriculum, choices about specific artists, artworks, artifacts, and cultures may best be left in very general terms as guidelines rather than specific requirements. As an example of a general guideline for choosing artworks, artists, and artifacts, the curriculum might specify an emphasis on contemporary art and artmaking practices found in Western and non-Western cultures with meaningful connections to past artistic practices and artworks. Specific choices would be left to individual teachers. A more specific approach would specify artworks, artifacts, cultures, time periods, and artmaking practices to be studied.

Regardless of how specifically or generally the art curriculum poses requirements for selecting artists, artworks, artifacts, and cultures for study, specific criteria should guide one's choices. These decisions often begin, quite naturally, at the intuitive level but eventually need to be connected to specific criteria within the curriculum. In Chapter 3, we proposed two simple criteria, *relevancy* and *diversity*, to guide curriculum choices. Relevancy was related to student interests and needs, contemporary culture, and important art learning. Diversity was linked to the given possibilities for categories under consideration. The argument for making curriculum choices about artists, artworks, artifacts, and cultures put forth in Chapter 3 contended that it is the application to specific cases which has import and develops deeper understandings of concepts and principles. Taking the time to question how particular artists, artworks, artifacts, and cultures relate to a specific student population, how they correlate with other curriculum selections and overall options, how they stimulate specific key art understandings and inquiry, and how they connect with enduring ideas will benefit the depth and breadth of the art curriculum and will avoid a hit-or-miss approach to art learning.

Looking Back

Author Cynthia Freeland related that Scottish philosopher David Hume and German philosopher Emmanuel Kant both believed that some works of art are better than others and some people have better taste. How did they account for this? Freeland describes the different approaches the philosophers assumed to justify their beliefs. Hume felt that people of education and experience can reach a consensus and set a "standard of taste" that is universal. Freeland contrasts Hume's beliefs with those of Kant, who also sought universal standards but more of beauty than taste. Instead of the intersubjectivity Hume advocated, Kant believed that judgments of beauty were grounded in the real world.

Source: C. Freeland, *But Is It Art?* (Oxford: Oxford University Press, 2001), pp. 8–14.

FAQs

What is art?

Philosopher George Dickie theorized that art is "any artifact . . . which has had conferred upon it the status of candidate for appreciation by some person or persons acting on behalf of a certain social institution (the art world)." Dickie labeled this the "institutional theory of art." Thus, the criteria for what is and is not art does not depend upon the work itself but rather the social institutions of a particular time period.

Source: George Dickie quoted in Cynthia Freeland, *But Is It Art?* (Oxford: Oxford University Press, 2001).

Looking Forward

Contemporary art emerges from a different aesthetic tradition than the formalism of Kant; in fact, postmodernism is often referred to as an anti-aesthetic tradition. Postmodern artists resist notions of beauty and formal allure, preferring to delve into social, cultural, and political issues. Remarks contemporary artist Rirkrit Tiravanija, "My work is about looking at the essential and what's essential more than survival."

Tiravanija designs rooms for communication and interaction, which he creates within the gallery space. In his first exhibitions, he installed a temporary kitchen where food was served and he interacted over the meal with viewers. Here the actions of viewers became a part of the work itself. In two other works, Tiravanija installed a set of drums for viewers to play and rehearsed a puppet play with young people.

Clearly, aesthetic theory based in formalism would have little relevance for interpreting and judging Tiravanija's work. More appropriate would be contextualist theories concerned with the social and cultural significance of artworks.

Source: Y. Dziewior, "Rirkrit Tiravanija." In *Art Now*, ed. Burkhard Riemschnieder (New York: Taschen, 2001), pp. 162–63.

Notes

1   O. Gude, "Rubrics for a Quality Art Curriculum," UIC Spiral Art Education (http://www.uic.edu/classes/ad/ad382/sites/AEA/AEA_02/AAEA02a.html).

2   M. Barkan, "Curriculum Problems in Art Education." In E. L. Mattil (ed.), *A Seminar in Art Education for Research and Curriculum Development* (University Park, PA: Pennsylvania State University, 1966), pp. 240–55.

3   A. Efland, "The Spiral and the Lattice: Changes in Cognitive Learning Theory with Implications for Art Education," *Studies in Art Education* 36, no. 3 (1995): pp. 136–53.

4   Ibid., pp. 146–53.

5   R. Prawat, "Teachers' Beliefs about Teaching and Learning: A Constructivist Perspective," *American Journal of Education* (May 1992), pp. 386–88.

6   Ibid., p. 387.

7   Ibid.

8   Ibid.

9   Terry Barrett, personal communication, April 2002.

10 The TETAC unit was created by Deborah George and Paula Flohr, at Sheldon High School in Sacramento, California.

11 R. Prawat,"Promoting Access to Knowledge, Strategy, and Disposition in Students: A Research Synthesis," *Review of Educational Research* 59, no. 1 (Spring 1989), pp. 1–41.

12 R. Glaser, "Education and Thinking: The Role of Knowledge," *American Psychologist* 39 (1984), pp. 93–104; S. W. Russ, *Affect & Creativity* (Mahwah, NJ: Lawrence Erlbaum Associates, Inc., 1993); and E. D. Hirsch Jr., "Seeking Depth and Breadth in the Curriculum," *Educational Leadership* (October 2001).

13 The TETAC unit was developed and implemented by Nancy Lilly at Lusher Alternative School and Ann Rowson Love at The Ogden Museum of Southern Art in New Orleans, 2001.

14 J. Poesch, "Will Henry Stevens (1881–1949)." In *Will Henry Stevens* (Greenville, NC: Greenville County Museum of Art, 1987).

15 J. R. Gruber, Director, The Ogden Museum of Southern Art, University of New Orleans, Louisiana, unpaginated.

16 J. Poesch, "Will Henry Stevens (1881–1949)," p. 4.

17 R. Arnheim, *The Genesis of a Painting: Picasso's Guernica* (Berkley, CA: University of California Press, 1962), p. 10.

18 B. Marden, "Brice Marden, Artist." In *Inside the Art World: Conversations with Barbaralee Diamondstein* (New York: Rizzoli, 1994), p. 171.

19 S. R. Walker and M. Mace, "Toward an Understanding of Creativity through a Qualitative Appraisal of Contemporary Art Making." *Creativity Journal* 10, nos. 2/3, 265–78; J. W. Getzels and M. Csikszentmihalyi, *The Creative Vision: A Longitudinal Study of Problem Finding in Art* (New York: John Wiley & Sons, 1976).

20 The TETAC unit was developed and implemented by Deborah George and Paula Flohr at Sheldon High School in Sacramento, California.

21 Marilyn G. Stewart, *Thinking Through Aesthetics* (Worcester, MA: Davis Publications, 1997).

22 The TETAC unit was developed and implemented by Deborah Kippley at Tara Heights Elementary School in Papillion, Nebraska.

Helping Students Learn: Instruction

"You have to take enough time to get kids deeply involved in something they can think about in lots of different ways. "
　—Howard Gardner

After discussing what they know about natural disasters and how nature can sometimes be powerful and unpredictable, a class of third graders views a reproduction of *The Great Wave* by the Japanese artist Hokusai. The teacher has the students look silently at the artwork for a few minutes and then asks them to consider a series of questions. "Why do you think the artist chose this subject to depict?" "How do you think the people in the small boat are feeling?" "How has the artist shown the power of nature?" With these and additional questions, she directs their attention to the overall mood of the image and the ways that the artist has used lines, shapes, and colors to suggest the mood and story told by the woodcut print.

The students have some prior knowledge of the power and unpredictability of nature and of many kinds of natural disasters, since these are themes studied in their science curriculum. In language arts, they have been reading a story about the *Titanic* and another one about Pompeii, the city destroyed by the eruption of a volcano. In this large-group discussion about the Hokusai woodcut print, the teacher asks her students to compare the situation on the *Titanic* with the one that Hokusai described in his artwork.

She concludes the discussion by asking students to share with the class the questions they have about the artwork and the artist. As she lists their questions on chart paper, she continues with prompts, and finally has them consider questions that they would like to ask the artist, imagining that he could come to visit their class. The students will return to their list of questions about the print and the artist in their next lesson.

5.1 Katsushika Hokusai, The Great Wave at Kanagawa. *From "36 Views of Mount Fuji," 1830–32. Nishiki-e color woodblock print on paper 9.76" x 14.29" (24.8 x 36.3 cm). Photo by Harry Bréjat. Musee des Arts Asiatiques-Guimet, Paris, France. Réunion des Musées Nationaux/Art Resource, NY.*

In the next lesson, the teacher reviews the questions raised at the end of the previous session. In order to help students discover answers to their many questions, she provides small reading groups with one of three readings—an article about Hokusai from a book of biographies, an article about the artist from a book on the lives of artists, and an article about Japan. After the students read their assigned reading, one student records what the group believes are the three or four main ideas. These ideas are shared with the whole class as the teacher records them on chart paper.

When asked to create "clusters" of these main ideas, the students organize their ideas into three main groups—ideas about the artist as a person, about the art that Hokusai created, and about the influence of Japan's environment on Hokusai's art. They will use these ideas as they write their own illustrated biographies of the artist.

Varieties of Experience Supporting Unit Foundations

The two lessons described in the preceding pages are part of an integrated unit based on the enduring idea "humans and nature: our awareness of and experience with the unpredictability of nature." The important idea related to art is that artists often show how people are affected by the unpredictability of nature. In subsequent lessons, students will consider more artworks by Hokusai. They will use a Venn diagram to compare Hokusai's work with *Tornado Over Kansas* by the American Regionalist artist John Steuart Curry. After viewing Hokusai's *A Sudden Gust of Wind at Ejiri,* they will create their own block prints that show the effects of wind on places with which they are familiar—the schoolyard, the street where they live, and so on.

Finally, the students will view and discuss a billboard beer advertisement that appropriates a Hokusai image, considering the changes to the artwork in this new context. They will divide into groups to consider questions such as, "Why was Hokusai's print chosen for a billboard advertisement?" and "Should advertisers be able to take a well-known work of art and use it to sell a product like beer?" Their discussions culminate in a debate on this issue. Eventually, the students will create another print, this time drawing upon what they have learned in their science classes about natural disasters, to show their own version of the effects of the unpredictability of nature. They will reflect on their learning in writing, and their writing will accompany their artworks in the Fine Arts Festival held in their school.

The third-grade unit of study was written by Jeannie Courter, along with several teacher consultants, at Carriage Elementary School in Citrus Heights, California. In addition to the various experiences described here, the students wrote letters to parents telling them about what they had learned, kept journals and shared their entries with peer partners, wrote critical essays, completed reflection worksheets, and created preliminary sketches for their prints. Much of their work provided evidence of what they were learning; that is, it functioned as a way for them and their teacher to assess the extent to which they learned what they were intended to learn. Large-group and small-group discussions were held periodically throughout the unit, and students were consistently encouraged to make connections between what they were learning in their art class with what they were learning in other content areas. Needless to say, they were busy!

What is important to note is that not only were they active but they were engaged in a variety of experiences designed by the teacher to assist them in

Five Key Art Understandings

- Art is a purposeful human endeavor.

- Art attains value, purpose, and meaning from the personal, social, and cultural dimensions of life.

- Art raises philosophical issues and questions.

- Artworks are objects for interpretation.

- Change is fundamental to art.

5.2 As students explore materials for their expressive potential, they investigate ways to create meaning in their studio work. Photo by Nancy Walkup.

developing deep understandings. The unit foundations were established early on, and the enduring ideas, key concepts, and unit and lesson objectives provided the focus for lesson development. In conceptualizing and writing the unit of study, Ms. Courter kept these unit foundations at the forefront, allowing them to guide her in planning instruction.

Teaching for Deep Understanding

This chapter focuses on instruction. In Chapter 4 we proposed that the content of art not be construed as a series of facts or skills, but rather as "key art understandings" that are complex and are deeply understood through repeated instruction in multiple contexts throughout the K–12 curriculum. We proposed that establishing a set of such understandings is paramount in developing curriculum, that they represent a conceptual framework for art knowledge that will ground the curriculum and guide planners in selecting enduring ideas, key concepts, and essential questions at the heart of each unit of study within the curriculum. In setting forth our notion of content, we included the practices of inquiry that inform art criticism, art history, artmaking, and aesthetics. In doing so, we recognize the complex and overlapping ways in which one constructs key art understandings. One increasingly integrates such understandings through an investigation of the origins and traditions of art within culture; an investigation of the various meanings conveyed through specific artworks; an investigation of the world, self, and others through artmaking; and an investigation of the range of philosophical questions and issues that emerge when one seriously engages in such work.

Since investigation is the avenue by which one constructs deep understandings, the classroom must be considered the locus for inquiry. In planning instruction, the teacher as facilitator attempts to bring students and new knowledge together in meaningful ways that "hook" students through engaging and thought-provoking experiences. The classroom community is a community of inquirers who value questioning, reflection, collaboration, sharing of findings, and the application to real-life situations of what is known. In our attempt to create such communities of inquirers, where authentic inquiry is valued over specific facts and skills, we need to consider how students learn but, more important, how students develop deep understandings. A few important factors influence and enhance this process.

The Right Stuff: Key Factors That Influence the Learning Experience

The old adage "We teach students, not subjects," like many slogans, carries with it important implications. The most beautifully designed lesson, filled with important content and well-crafted instructional strategies and resources, can easily fall flat when it is provided for students who are not ready for it or for whom it is a repeat of something they have already learned. We need to know what our students know about the topics we intend to address. In the lesson in which students critically view the Hokusai print for the first time, the teacher was aware that her students were familiar with natural disasters and had studied the unpredictability of nature in their science curriculum. Knowing also that they were familiar with the story of the *Titanic,* she was able to prepare an activity in which students would compare it to the story described in Hokusai's print. Their engagement with the artwork extended their understanding of the concepts addressed in science, and their prior knowledge allowed them to more deeply understand the import of the scene depicted in the print.

Bumper-Sticker Questions

In an eighth-grade unit entitled "Not Just a Pretty Picture: Depicting Conflict through Art," Texas teachers Keri Huse and Barbara Krishman focused attention on the importance of student questioning. Throughout the unit, students were encouraged to post their questions on "bumper stickers"—3" x 8" strips of paper. The questions were then taped to or pinned to a large space on the wall dedicated to this purpose. When students found definitions or other answers to their questions, they recorded them on additional stickers and attached them near the original questions. This strategy encourages students first to articulate their questions and second, to investigate their own questions and those of their peers.

Helping Students Build Upon What They Know

In a fifth-grade unit entitled "Thriving on Affection: The Enduring Love Affair Between People and Their Pets," a lesson objective was for students to demonstrate how artists have shown affectionate human-pet relationships in different times and in different cultures.*

After engaging students in a discussion about their own experiences with pets, the teacher asked students to collect advertisements and cartoons that show people and their pets. They then critically considered the collected items along with selected artworks from a variety of time periods and cultures that show human-pet relationships. Students were then asked to arrange the artworks and collected items in chronological order and to select two artworks that they would like to know more about. Students engaged in online research about the artworks and the social and historical contexts in which they were made.

Drawing upon their research, the students completed a timeline that placed their selected artworks within a context of significant world and/or cultural events and, when possible, events in the artist's life.

*This unit was designed by Kelly Smith of Oakhurst Elementary School, Fort Worth ISD, Fort Worth, Texas.

Planning for New Knowledge Construction

Instructional planning must consider not only what students already know but the new knowledge that we wish them to construct. Our planning must ensure that students will be able to make connections between what they already know (their prior knowledge) and what we want them to know and understand. An instructional technique known as K-W-L, created by D. M. Ogle,[1] can be used to assist students in constructing meaning. Teachers ask students what they already know (K), what they want to learn (W), and, after investigating, what they have learned (L). This sequence can be modified so that what students have learned is replaced by asking how students will learn what they want to learn—what kind of investigation would be appropriate. Clearly, this can be followed by returning to the original questions and reflecting on what has been learned through the investigation.

Teaching for Student Relevance

In planning instruction, it is important to consider how meaningful the learning experience is from the students' perspective. The various strategies employed by the teacher in our model lessons were designed to build upon students' other experiences—in and out of school. Their work with the Hokusai print and the other artworks tapped into the students' experiences in their science and language arts classes, but they were also asked to consider the effects of nature on the schoolyard or other familiar places outside of their own school. In presenting an opportunity for students to think philosophically, the teacher used a local billboard as a catalyst, rather than simply asking students if there could be issues involved when artworks are appropriated for use in other contexts.

Devising an "Entrance Strategy"

In planning instruction, it is essential that the teacher consider how to engage students' interest at the outset. Ms. Courter began her lesson by asking students to tell what they knew about natural disasters. Knowing that they had been studying natural disasters in their science and language arts classes was important, as well as knowing that these students were likely to enjoy sharing what they knew. In showing students a copy of the Hokusai print and asking them to talk about it, she was employing a strategy that is often used by art teachers to generate interest and focus student attention on ideas central to a lesson. Students like to look at artworks and enjoy sharing their ideas about what they see. Her questions helped the students to make personal connections to the artwork—another important way to engage student interest. When planning instruction, teachers need to consider how they will enter into an investigation of the enduring ideas, key concepts, and essential questions.

Knowledge Under Construction

We have come to recognize that as learners, we actually construct knowledge in a dynamic process through which we build upon prior knowledge as we experience the world. We reformulate and refilter our previous understandings. The key question that serves as the basis of constructivism is "What does that mean?" As instructional planners, we need to consider ways to engage students so that this question emerges—and that it emerges from them.

Suggesting Avenues of Inquiry

When we take seriously the notion that students construct rather than receive knowledge, then inquiry-based instruction is the methodology we employ to assist them. The teacher's role is that of a guide or

Point-of-Entry Activity

In an third-grade unit entitled "Unsolved Mysteries: Amazing Parallels between Ancient Egyptian and Mayan Art," art teacher Judi Short of Greenbriar Elementary School, Fort Worth, Texas, engaged student interest with the following strategy:

After explaining the terms "archaeologist" and "dig," the teacher told students that they would pretend to be archaeologists traveling to the site of an imaginary dig. While locating the areas on a large class map, the teacher explained that half of the class would travel to the Egyptian desert and the other half would travel to the Mayan jungles of lower Mexico. Students were provided with detailed maps of the areas to which they were to travel, along with reproductions of an Egyptian tomb painting, *Nebamun Hunting Birds*, and a Mayan relief sculpture, *Presentation of Captives to a Mayan Ruler*, that they would "find" in their archaeological dig. Students received a handout with a series of questions for them to consider as they carefully described the artworks they were to have found on their site. Following their investigations, students engaged in a large class discussion in which they identified features of the artworks that were unique to each site and those that were similar. This point-of-entry activity served to heighten student interest at the beginning of the unit of study.

Extended Group Membership and Inquiry

In a high school interdisciplinary unit entitled "Man's Mechanical Journey," honors physics and advanced art students were told that they would be working together in teams to design and construct a quality artistic product that demonstrates important physical principles of energy conservation, motion, and machine elements.* The teams were formed at the beginning of the unit and stayed together for its duration. Each team included one member designated as the art "expert" and two members designated as the physics/engineering "experts." It was made clear that all students were responsible for the artistic and physics elements, but that the experts were to be used as subject-specific resources. The teams engaged in a variety of activities, including a discussion of questions such as, "When does an engineered product become a work of art?" in which they considered, for example, an automobile as a product engineered for function, yet also designed to be aesthetically pleasing. As part of their work toward the creation of their product, they also viewed and discussed many examples of kinetic sculpture and kept a team journal and a portfolio detailing their problem-solving process, research, and planning.

*This unit was designed by Kim McGreevey and Charles Warner, Woodland High School, Woodland, California.

facilitator whose job is to provide opportunities for students to raise and address questions—a problem presenter, initially, with the goal of having students present their own problems eventually. Students become researchers and problem solvers. As facilitator, the teacher provides a conceptual context—the enduring ideas and key concepts—for generating questions. In addition, the teacher helps students identify questions that are meaningful within that context.

In examining the Hokusai artwork, the students were encouraged to list their questions about the artwork and the artist. To help them generate these questions, the teacher suggested that they imagine that the artist would be visiting the class. This scenario was an aid to the students' development of questions. The list of questions was referred to as the students worked in groups to categorize the kinds of things that they wanted to learn. With these categories in mind, they read about the artist and Japanese

5.3 When students compare and contrast, they practice critical-thinking skills. Photo by Nancy Walkup.

culture, focusing their attention upon information that they had already deemed as important.

Focusing on Process

The goal of inquiry-based instruction is for students to become engaged in a process of learning that can be replicated. We want students to learn how to learn. Students will create products (oral presentations, artworks, essays, performances, etc.), but these are indicators of the process, not the primary purpose of the learning experience. Teachers can assist students in recognizing and reflecting upon the process through which they have learned by asking such questions as "What did you learn from this process?" "What did you do?" "What was particularly helpful or not helpful?" "What did you learn that you can use in future inquiry?" Especially in art classrooms, the focus has tended to be on the finished product. In an art program that centralizes ideas and knowledge construction, process is deemed equally, if not more, important than product.

Practicing Needed Skills

To teach for deep understanding is not to ignore the fact that students require proficiency in a range of skills. These skills might be technical or practical as well as cognitive. In preparing for instruction, we need to identify the various skills required, as well as the level at which we want students to develop their expertise. Skill proficiency requires practice and connection to prior skills. Instructional strategies can be designed to provide for such connections and practice.

Application of Knowledge

If students are to take an active role in developing new knowledge, they will need to have learning experiences that require them to appropriately take

5.4 While constructing visual forms, students can articulate their reasons for making artistic decisions. Photo by Marilyn Stewart.

Creating for Another Audience

In the following examples, when assigning work for students, teachers asked them to consider an audience beyond their teacher and peers. Note the format used in assigning these tasks.*

Analyzing an Artwork Task

Goal: Your task is to analyze a work of art for personal and cultural content.

Role: You are part of a team of student art historians that has been asked by the Joslyn Art Museum to make a preliminary analysis of a work of art for its cultural and personal content.

Audience: Joslyn Art Museum staff and the general public.

Situation: The challenge involves dealing with a mysterious artwork that has been found hidden in a museum vault. Student art historians have been asked to analyze this work for social and personal content before the professional team of art historians arrives to conduct a more thorough analysis.

Product: You will need to write a preliminary report that will consist of one paragraph of your findings.

Standard: Your paragraph needs to include at least two things that are of a personal nature and at least three things that are of cultural or social significance to that time period. You might observe various aspects of the work, including clothing, jewelry or other accessories, tools, hobbies, theme, pose, general surroundings, subject matter, toys, pets, evidence of wealth or poverty, furniture style, architecture, and so on as we discussed when viewing the other artworks in Lesson One.

*These tasks were part of the third-grade unit "Preserving Memories," designed by Lois Rongisch of Tara Heights Elementary School, Papillon, Nebraska.

Self-Portrait Task

Goal: Your task is to make a self-portrait with symbols of meaningful memories surrounding you in the background that communicates to others who you are.

Role: You are a participant putting together a family album.

Audience: The target audience is your extended family and your family for generations to come.

Situation: The context you find yourself in is that each family member will design a page for the family album that is a self-portrait. The portrait will be a visual likeness surrounded by symbols that communicate who you are.

Product: You will create a page for the family album that is a self-portrait that contains symbols/images of things that are important to you.

Photo-Essay Task

Goal: Your task is to make a photo-essay of an event in your life told in story form.

Role: You are a pen pal to a child your age from another country.

Audience: The target audience is your pen pal and family.

Situation: The context you find yourself in is that your pen pal and family have asked you to put together a series of pictures that tell a story about what your life is like in America.

Product: You will create a photo-essay of an event in your life that depicts a theme (buying a Christmas tree, celebrating a special occasion, a day with your family, etc.) along with a narrative under each picture describing each sequence.

knowledge learned in one context and use it in another. In planning instruction, teachers need to provide opportunities for students to apply what they have learned. Of course, this is best accomplished when they apply new knowledge to real-life situations. In the TETAC project, we emphasized the importance of having students apply their new knowledge in situations in which the "audience" for their work is other than the teacher and fellow students. For example, students create such things as learning guides for another class, bulletin boards, or other public displays.

Organizing Instruction
Students need to move from simple to complex understandings—from basic awareness to insightful evaluation of knowledge. The enduring ideas, key concepts, and essential questions provide the overall conceptual structure for the unit of instruction. All instruction must be planned so that these ideas and questions are increasingly understood. In addition, instruction must be sequenced so that each learning experience builds upon the one preceding it.

Broadcasting Assessment Expectations
When providing students with tasks to complete, whether it be, for example, an oral or written interpretation of an artwork, a group project that addresses the historical context in which an artwork was produced, or an individual artmaking assignment, we need to help students understand what a successful completion of the task would include. Both teacher and students need to be aware of how the specific task connects to the enduring ideas, key concepts, and objectives of the unit of study. In addition, all need to be aware of how the task relates to the particular lesson objectives. In order for students to perform well, they need to be aware of why they are being asked to do so—how this particular learning

activity will move them toward the understandings that are central to the unit. In addition, they need to be aware of what constitutes exemplary, essential, and partial levels of achievement relative to the task. Chapter 6 will provide a more thorough examination of the role of assessment in curriculum planning, but it is important to recognize here that student awareness of what is expected of them is a key factor that affects learning.

The Basics: Considerations in Planning Instruction
Longstanding tradition in curriculum planning organizes curriculums into units of instruction or what some refer to as units of study. An important way to think about a unit is to think of it as a conceptual whole. As explained in Chapter 3, an enduring idea provides the broad conceptual framework for the unit. Tied to this enduring idea are several key concepts, essential questions, and unit objectives. Together with a rationale for addressing the enduring idea and related concepts, questions, and objectives, these provide the focus for planning. We have referred to these as the unit foundations.

A unit is not necessarily connected to a specific period of time, but it can be conceived in terms of time. For example, some curriculum planners use their school's academic year breakdown into terms or quarters as a way of planning timing for units of study. In this book, we consider a unit of study more in terms of ideas and the time it takes to investigate them. A unit conceivably could extend for an entire academic year, depending on the depth of investigation planned, but we are not prescribing this. Suffice it to say that an academic year, in most cases, would consist of several units of instruction.

Units of study are further divided into lessons. Again, a lesson is a conceptual entity, not necessarily

Careful Planning for Sequence

In designing a unit entitled "There Is Still-Life in Middle School Language Arts!" teacher Elaine Nicoloso of Florida State University School, Tallahassee, planned three different ways in which students would encounter and discuss artworks by artist William Harnett. The second and third encounters built upon the first. Note, also, that the teacher included questions for discussion as part of her planning.

In the first lesson, Nicoloso showed the students some of Harnett's realistic still-life paintings. She made a point to conceal any written information about the artworks and asked students to consider the works. She planned the following questions for the discussion:

1 How do you think these artworks were created? *(The paintings are so lifelike that some students might think that they are photographs.)*

2 What do you think about when you look at the painting?

3 What objects do you recognize in the painting?

4 What objects tend to recur in several paintings?

5 Why do you think this might be?

6 Why do you think the artist chose the objects in the painting?

7 What kind of person might use some of these objects?

8 Why do you think the artist placed the objects where he did?

9 What do you think is the most important part of the picture? Why?

10 What might some of the objects symbolize?

11 What do you think is good about the painting? Why do you think that?

12 How do you think the artist went about making this artwork?

13 What questions would you ask the artist who did this work?

14 On a scale of one to ten, how would you rate this work? Give reasons for your response.

After the large-group discussion, the teacher asked students to select one of the William Harnett paintings and, based on their observations, complete the questions on a worksheet titled "Art Detective," which contained questions similar to those asked of the whole group. This second activity built upon the first, which functioned as a model for students as they worked independently.

In the next lesson, the teacher provided students with information about the artist and his life and painting techniques. Students learned that the artist included objects in many of his paintings that have a common theme about the inevitable passage of time, reflecting a preoccupation with mortality and the fleeting rewards of material wealth. She had the students work in small groups and return to the same artworks and consider them in light of this new information. Again, she prepared questions (and possible answers) in advance, this time to go along with specific artworks. For example, for the Harnett work *Music and Literature*, she planned the following:

1 Why do you think he included books and sheet music? (Music and literature help preserve the past.)

2 What do you notice about the condition of the books and the sheet music? (The books are worn with age and the music is stained and torn.)

3 Why do you think he included a candle almost completely burned down and snuffed out? (reminder of death)

4 What kind of mood is created by these objects and their arrangement? (melancholy, etc.)

linked to time. One lesson might, and often does, extend for more than one class period, for example. A lesson is typically organized around a set of ideas that are related to, but more specific than, the enduring idea, key concepts, and essential questions of the unit. Lessons typically are considered as parts of the whole, designed and organized to allow students to gain increasingly sophisticated understandings of the unit foundations.

In planning units and lessons, curriculum planners design strategies (sometimes referred to as activities or experiences) that will assist students in deepening their understanding of the unit foundations. In addition, such strategies are designed to address specific learning objectives outlined in the lesson plan. Strategies are designed with several things in mind—where they fit within the sequence of strategies within the unit and lesson, the content or skills to be learned, the developmental levels of the students, and the extent to which they will "hook" or engage the interests and imaginations of the learners.

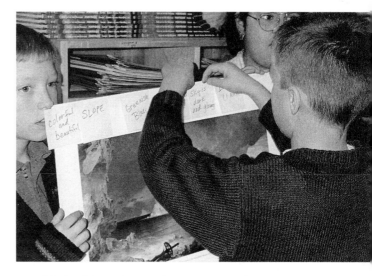

5.5 While describing and interpreting an artwork, students attach their descriptions around the edge of the reproduction. Photo by Nancy Walkup.

Unit and Lesson Objectives

We discussed unit objectives in Chapter 3 as a restatement, in a general way, of the enduring idea, key concepts, and essential questions that have been identified. We explained that unit objectives are broader than lesson objectives and noted that a unit of study might have a just a few objectives, but that the lessons within the unit typically would have more, and that these would be more specific than those identified for the unit.

Unit objectives, further, are stated to indicate the kinds of understandings that students would have as a result of their engagement in the unit of study. When skills are listed, they are stated in broader terms than the skills addressed in the various lessons. Lesson objectives are more specific in indicating what students will know and be able to do.

Objectives and Assessment

In planning a unit of study, we need to consider what would count as evidence that students do, indeed, understand the enduring ideas and key concepts, and that they are able to demonstrate the skills identified in the unit objectives. If we have deemed an idea and some key concepts as significant for students to understand, then it makes sense that we would also plan ways for students to demonstrate that they have developed these understandings. We need to consider, then, how learning or understanding will be demonstrated and assessed. One way to proceed is to describe several ways through which students might demonstrate their understanding and skills. Often referred to as end-of-unit performance tasks, these activities provide focus for the lessons and accompanying instructional strategies. With the end in sight, curriculum planners are better able to determine how students should move through a series of lessons.

Alignment of Unit Goals, Lesson Objectives, and State Standards

The objectives or goals in the unit described at the beginning of this chapter were as follows:

- Students will understand that artists can show the unpredictability of nature.
- Students will understand that they, too, can show the unpredictability of nature through their own art.

The learning objectives for the various lessons in the unit were more specific than the overall unit objectives. Note the following from Lesson One:

- Students will understand the artwork (Hokusai's *The Great Wave Off Kanagawa*) in the context of the unpredictability of nature and natural disasters.
- Students will explore the meaning of *The Great Wave Off Kanagawa*.

Lesson One objectives were also aligned with the following California Visual Arts Standards:

Standard 1. Artistic Perception—Processing, analyzing, and responding to sensory information through the language and skills unique to the visual arts.

Standard 4. Aesthetic Valuing—Responding to, analyzing, and making judgments about the visual arts.

Standard 5. Connections, Relations, and Applications—Connecting and applying what is learned in the visual arts to other arts forms, subject areas, and careers.*

*The unit on humans and nature, "Every Aspect of Nature Is Man's First Inspiration," was designed by Jeannie Courter with consultants Anne Youngs, Imelda Little, Becky Bachman, Rachel de Becker, Sherry Blevins, and Tina Montano of Carriage Elementary School, Citrus Heights, California.

Instructional planning involves the design of a series of activities that will prepare students to successfully engage in the end-of-unit performance task.

In planning lesson objectives and instructional strategies, then, the curriculum planners aim toward a deeper understanding of the enduring ideas, key concepts, and skills identified in unit objectives to be demonstrated in an end-of-unit performance task. In doing so, however, they identify specific knowledge and skills that will contribute to this deeper understanding. Specific lesson objectives should align with unit objectives. The planner must be able to show how students' work toward the learning outlined in the lesson objectives is connected to a deeper understanding of the unit's enduring ideas and key concepts. Assessment is important in planning lessons as well. The principle is the same: If we believe that certain specific knowledge and skills are important for students to have, then we need to design ways for them to demonstrate what they have learned. Lessons will include opportunities for students and teachers to demonstrate and assess progress. In the next chapter, we will discuss the kinds of assessment that planners might include in the context of lessons.

The Role of Standards

In identifying unit and lesson objectives, curriculum planners pay attention to standards. The National Visual Arts Standards have served as a starting point in the development of standards at the state and local levels. Generally, what is included in the national standards is also included in other sets of standards that have been developed. State and local standards might include more specific language or additional content, but the spirit of most content standards at the state and local levels is consistent with the notion of content explained in Chapter 4. This means that curriculum in the arts that is consistent with national, state, or local standards will include opportunities for students to create artworks but also to understand them in historical, cultural, and critical contexts. School district guidelines vary in terms of the degree to which curriculum planners ought to align their arts curricula to specific sets of standards. However, when planning units of instruction, planners generally are able to align unit and lesson objectives to the standards deemed important within their school districts. Again, depending on local guidelines, curriculum planners can use standards as a central or peripheral step in the curriculum design process.

While standards generally outline what students should know and be able to do, they do not address the sorts of ideas that we identify as the "key art understandings." These understandings are often implied by the standards, but they are not stated explicitly. Accordingly, the standards do not put forward a set of enduring ideas such as we are promoting as foundational for curriculum planning. We suggest that enduring ideas are much broader than the specific knowledge and skills identified in the standards. Enduring ideas of the sort we propose throughout this book provide the overarching "umbrella" through which learning identified in the standards can be addressed.

In the TETAC project, teachers worked with the TETAC Curriculum Guidelines to generate enduring ideas, key concepts, and essential questions and were often able to make direct connections to the standards deemed appropriate within their school districts. Additionally, when creating more specific lesson objectives, they routinely made direct connections to the standards for which they were responsible.

How Will I Teach That? Instructional Strategies

Once the work of identifying enduring ideas, key concepts, and essential questions has been completed

Objectives and Assessment

In Lesson One of the humans and nature unit described at the beginning of this chapter, the teacher designed the following formative assessment in relation to the lesson objectives mentioned above:

- Students will write on a sheet of paper or in a journal to the following prompt: I would like to tell my parents three things about Hokusai's *The Great Wave Off Kanagawa* today when I go home. The three things are the following:

- After students have completed writing, they turn to a partner and share what they have written. For homework, students are instructed to share the woodcut with their parents and to remember to describe the woodcut as they tell about it.*

*The unit "Every Aspect of Nature Is Man's First Inspiration" was designed by Jeannie Courter with consultants Anne Youngs, Imelda Little, Becky Bachman, Rachel de Becker, Sherry Blevins, and Tina Montano of Carriage Elementary School, Citrus Heights, California.

5.6 Teachers may wish to work together to make sure that lesson objectives and instructional strategies align with unit objectives, standards, and, ultimately, the enduring ideas and key concepts of the unit.

and a set of unit objectives has been outlined, curriculum planners must ask the question "How will students demonstrate that they understand what it is that we wish them to understand?" As mentioned previously, this results in the design of end-of-unit performance tasks—tasks that provide evidence of student learning.

The next step is to plan ways for students to engage in the investigation of the essential questions, and thereby to be introduced to the enduring ideas and key concepts of the unit. This step consists of designing and sequencing strategies or activities that will move the students from where they currently are in terms of knowledge and understanding to the place where they will demonstrate their more sophisticated understanding through the performance task.

Though we by no means present an exhaustive set of specific instructional strategies here, we do provide a few ways to consider instructional strategies and offer some guidelines for designing instruction. We suggest that arts teachers also talk with classroom teachers about instructional strategies that they use in teaching various subjects. We have found, for example, that many of the strategies designed for teaching in language arts, social studies, science, and math can be useful for teaching in the visual and performing arts. This is particularly true when those strategies include an emphasis on student inquiry and problem solving.

Selecting Content for Relevance and Diversity

Sometimes it makes sense, early in the process of curriculum planning, to select artworks, objects, or sites that, when considered carefully for their meaning, will assist students in developing an understanding of the enduring ideas and key concepts of the unit. As we suggested in Chapter 4, an enduring idea can be developed through a wide range of artworks and

objects. As we also stated, there are so many possible artworks, objects, and sites from which to select that teachers cannot hope to introduce students to all that exist. We need to make choices. Reasons for selecting some over others vary. For example, a curriculum planner might know that in previous units students were introduced to artworks from a time period or culture other than their own and so decide to introduce students in the current unit to contemporary art from their own culture. In Chapter 3 we proposed two simple criteria, relevancy and diversity, to guide such choices. What is important here, as we consider the design of instructional strategies, is that the artworks, objects, or sites selected for use in a unit of instruction can often inform the decisions we make about instructional strategies. Activities for viewing and interpreting architecture, for example, may be different from those designed for viewing and interpreting a contemporary installation or a painting from another century. As we create strategies, we are guided by our unit foundations and the kinds of artworks, objects, or sites that we have selected to aid our understanding of the enduring ideas and key concepts.

Guidance from the Art Content

For guidance in designing instructional strategies, we look to the inquiry concepts and principles associated with the practice of artmaking, art criticism, art history, and aesthetics. As we approach the planning of artmaking experiences for our students, we ask, "How can we assist students in making meaningful artworks tied to the ideas and concepts of this unit?" As we approach the planning of inquiry associated with art criticism, we ask, "How can we assist students in interpreting and making judgments about artworks, objects, and sites?" Informing our planning of instructional strategies associated with art-historical inquiry

A Sampling of Instructional Strategies Used by TETAC Teachers

- **Body Movement.** Use of body movements to emphasize key concepts.

- **Brainstorming.** Participants "storm their brains" for ideas related to a topic or a problem. All ideas are treated equally, with no initial judgments as to their merit.

- **Buzz Sessions.** Small group discussions.

- **Collaborative Learning.** Students work together to address a problem or task, often with assigned roles.

- **Graphic Organizers** such as Venn diagrams and concept maps to organize important ideas. One teacher used "hula-hoops" as Venn diagrams.

- **Group Writing** in response to artworks or as reflections about group process.

- **KWHL Charts.** Students state what they Know, Want to know, How they will find out, and what they have Learned.

- **Learning Centers or Stations** through which students explore resources designed by the teacher or, in some cases, by the students for other (sometimes younger) learners.

- **Learning Packets.** Materials typically created by the teacher but at times created by students, through which learners explore information and concepts related to the unit ideas and concepts.

- **Letter Writing,** sometimes to parents; other times to public officials, through which students are encouraged to think about a specific issue and audience.

- **Listen-Think-Pair-Share.** A strategy through which students listen to questions, individually think about their response, discuss their ideas with a partner, and then share their ideas with the class.

- **Manipulatives.** Objects or word/statement cards used to assist students in exploring ideas and/or issues.

- **Pair Problem Solving.** One member of the pair is the "thinker" who thinks aloud in trying to solve a problem or address an issue. The partner is the "listener" who considers the "thinker's" ideas and provides feedback.

- **Panel Discussions** in which students form a panel of "experts" on a particular topic and present to others.

- **Poetic forms.** A variety of different poetic forms for use in interpreting artworks or summarizing important learning.

- **Problem-based Scenarios.** Hypothetical or "real" situations, embedded with problems for students to address; also used for assessment tasks.

- **Role-playing** and other forms of dramatization for discussing important issues, for interpreting artworks, for learning more about artists, etc. In one lesson, students assumed the role of something in an artwork and were interviewed by another student; in another lesson, students played the role of radio show hosts who described artworks on display.

- **Roundtable Discussions.** Like panel discussions through which students discuss a topic among themselves and share with an audience.

- **Sorting Activities.** Students sort objects and/or art reproductions into categories that are provided by the teacher or are created by the students.

- **Timelines.** Students create a visual record of their findings about the historical and cultural context for works of art, artists, styles of art, etc.

- **Videos, DVDs, PowerPoint Presentations, etc.,** for presenting information related to the ideas of a unit.

- **Web Quests.** A strategy through which students find, document and use information found on the Web.

- **Word Wall.** This is a designated place for placing words derived from group brainstorming or other kinds of discussions.

5.7 *In a workshop setting, teachers explore dance as a way to kinesthetically interpret artworks and, in this case, plan a collaborative dance piece based on the work of glass artist Dale Chihuly. Photo by Marilyn Stewart.*

are questions such as "How can we assist students in understanding the social, cultural, and historical contexts in which artworks, objects, and sites were created?" Finally, as we plan ways for students to engage in philosophical inquiry, we ask, "How can we assist them in their attempt to develop thoughtful and personally meaningful ideas about art and its role in society, in general?" As we plan curriculum, we attend to the inquiry associated with these several ways of knowing and thereby address what we have identified as key art understandings and, concurrently, the content of art.

We have stated that these areas of inquiry, or ways of knowing, are wonderfully complex and necessarily overlap in practice. We might plan a lesson in which all are intertwined as we guide students in deepening

their understanding of enduring ideas and key concepts. However, some lessons that we plan might have art criticism inquiry as a primary focus, while others might have artmaking, art-historical inquiry, or aesthetics as the primary focus.

Practice Makes Perfect

Each of the aforementioned areas of art inquiry involves application of specific skills, and because skill acquisition requires practice it makes sense to include opportunities for students to engage in that practice. This means, for example, that we don't include art-historical inquiry one time only in an arts curriculum. Instead, we come back to the skills of description and historical interpretation repeatedly throughout the K–12 program. In order to acquire the skills that they will take with them into adulthood, students require practice in describing and interpreting artworks, objects, and sites, and so we include instructional strategies designed to afford them this practice throughout the K–12 curriculum. This principle of repeated practice applies to skills in artmaking and aesthetics as well. In designing instructional strategies for a particular unit of instruction, we look to the areas of inquiry associated with a comprehensive engagement of art as potential ways for students to investigate and understand the enduring ideas and key concepts of the unit.

Considering Instructional Strategies in Broad Terms

One way to categorize instructional strategies is to think of them as either involving direct or indirect instruction. In order to move students to an understanding of significant ideas, concepts, and skills, it is often important for the teacher to provide information to students, demonstrate certain skill-based activities, model forms of inquiry or inner speech associated with reflective learning, provide explanations, and provide corrective feedback. This is direct instruction, as we are using the term. With direct instruction, the teacher assumes a central role in the classroom. This is consistent with more traditional notions of teaching whereby the teacher is seen as an expert who imparts information to the students. In the view of teaching that we are proposing in this book, direct instruction is coupled with indirect instruction. The challenge for the teacher is to determine when to move from this central position to the "coaching" position required for inquiry-based learning and when to move back again to the role of expert.

Indirect instruction, as we are employing the term, is when the teacher is engaged in guiding students in their own investigations, whether students are working independently or in groups. We know that students learn best when they are engaged actively in an instructional task, so in designing instructional strategies we aim to provide students with opportunities for such engagement.[2] We also know that learning is increased when students are assisted in organizing, storing, and retrieving knowledge.[3] Since our aim is to help students become independent, self-regulated learners, we need to design instructional strategies toward this end. Indirect instruction consists of the teacher setting up situations in which students will be the major producers of knowledge. This often means designing strategies that will guide students to raise questions and assist them in their investigations of these questions. It also often means that the teacher will back away from a central role in the classroom as students work independently or in groups.

Talking Points: Planning for Class Discussions
Class discussion is so basic and necessary an instructional strategy that sometimes teachers fail to

Teacher Reflection

The following is an excerpt from a teacher's reflection about an art history lesson she designed for her students.

"Lesson Three: Art History. I changed this lesson quite a bit after I did it with the class. While the class was doing this timeline lesson, I probably got the least energetic response from my students. Many students didn't even end up turning in this project. I knew I had to work on it. The timeline, which was supposed to focus on the life of Carmen Lomas Garza, Sandra Cisneros, and the Chicano movement, was mostly weak because I didn't have many sources of information to give to the groups. My students in the Chicano Studies class knew a lot more than I did about the Chicano movement and commented on how the sources I gave them were not very detailed or helpful.

"My first step was to get more information and to study the movement. Then I changed how the groups would work. Previously I had three people in a group, and each member received one of the topics. It was then their job to read the information on their topic and to chart it on the group's timeline. I think this failed essentially because even though students were sitting in groups, they were not working as a group because each was focusing on a different topic. This made for a lot of individual work with information that was not that appropriate.

"What did I do to change it? First, I gathered more research materials. Then I decided to give each group one topic. They now can work together to review the information and chart out a timeline. I added a presentation of the information and timeline because it is important that all students get the details on all of the topics. Then, to check for understanding, I included a prompt for the students to use in writing."

Source: Janet Parker, Woodland High School, Woodland, California.

Encouraging Discussion Contribution

It is often helpful to provide students with word cards or other manipulatives to assist them in talking about objects or works of art.

In a unit entitled "What Does a Friend Look Like? Friendship in Art," the teacher led the students in a discussion about the words, phrases, and traits that they think of when they think of friendship.* She asked the students to write their responses on small pieces of paper. Student responses included "caring," "friends are helpful," "friends like being together," and "friends have fun." The students placed their responses in a basket. They were then shown several reproductions of art that dealt with friendship. Each student selected a word or phrase from the basket and placed it near a given artwork. Students were asked to explain the connection between the art-work selected and the word or phrase. The teacher then led the students in a large-group discussion about the artworks.

*This unit was designed by Jennifer English, Marie Houran, and Michelle Mattoon of Mitchell Elementary School, Plano, Texas.

recognize the need to plan discussions. We have seen lesson plans, for example, in which the planners simply state something like "Discuss the artworks." In the model lesson with which we began this chapter, the teacher planned to lead the students in a large-group, or whole-class, discussion. In planning for this discussion, she listed the questions that she would ask the students and anticipated the kinds of answers that they would probably provide. She wanted to activate their prior knowledge about natural disasters and then to consider the subject matter and moods and feelings conveyed by the featured artwork. She knew that, as a strategy for generating questions, she would ask students to consider what they would ask the artist were it possible for him to come to the class and speak with them. Some class discussions are goal-oriented, such as this one. Others are more open-ended in that the teacher sincerely wants his or her students to grapple with a question or issue and cannot really anticipate the paths the discussion will take.

When planning for a large-group discussion, whether it is goal-oriented or open-ended, teachers should consider ways to encourage participation by all members of the group. To do this, the teacher can use a variety of strategies. For instance, the teacher can call on specific students and ask them their views on the topic. The teacher might pose possible answers to the initial question and ask students to indicate whether they agree or disagree with the statement and provide reasons for their views. A similar strategy is to provide all students with cards that contain various statements regarding the topic. The teacher can ask various students to read the statements on their cards and tell the class whether they agree or disagree and why. This strategy helps students overcome their hesitancy to enter into the discussion. Another strategy is to appoint a student to assume the role of discussion leader. In an attempt to move a discussion along, a teacher might suggest that the students gather together in small groups.

Talk Time: Working with Groups

Grouping, which is based on the assumption that learning is naturally a social act, has several advantages for the classroom teacher. As students work together, they talk among themselves. They hear from a variety of perspectives and thereby consider ideas or strategies that they might not generate on their own. These alternative views challenge the individual students to clarify their own ideas and thereby develop ownership that they might not have articulated without the group dynamic. Teachers make decisions about when to involve students as an entire class for instruction and when to involve them in smaller groups. Group size can vary from very small, such as when students work in pairs or triads, to larger groups. We want to provide opportunities for a range of viewpoints, on one hand, but want to avoid opportunities for individual students to get lost in the process. Accordingly, we have found that it is best to avoid groups of six or more.

One way to think about grouping is to consider the time allotted for group work. For instance, an informal group might be created when a teacher asks students to consider a question or idea with fellow students seated near them. This would be a short-lived group with very little structure. A more formal group might be formed to engage in a task or project that has a longer life. A teacher would need to consider more carefully the group composition and structure of the group. Some teachers create groups that last throughout an entire semester or academic year. These students develop a sense of pride in their group membership and accomplishments. They work on a variety of tasks as they occur within the curriculum.

Thinking Like a Coach

The teacher is the mediator of student learning, whether students are working independently or in groups. This means that the teacher intervenes, helping students to identify problems to investigate and projects on which to work. In the early stages of preparing students to identify their own problems and projects, the teacher will be actively involved in the problem-finding and project-description process. As students work, the teacher asks such questions as, "How are you going to approach this problem?" "What will you need to help you with this problem—what resources and/or materials will you need?" "What procedures will you follow?" "How will you know when the problem is solved or the project completed?" In modeling these questions for the students, the teacher is preparing them to be independent, self-regulated learners.

5.8 Students were encouraged to mimic the form of sculptures they encountered on a field trip. Photo by Marilyn Stewart.

Assigning Group Roles

In a lesson that introduced a unit entitled "Depicting Beauty," students were asked to work in small, collaborative groups to address the concepts of beauty and art.* They were introduced to two sets of terms, "big art/little art" and "big beauty/little beauty," and were given worksheets with a set of terms placed at opposite ends of a continuum. They were to consider a variety of objects and artworks and to discuss where they would place them on the continuum. They were also assigned the following collaborative learning roles:

1 **Discussion Leader:** focus the discussion; keep group members on track;

2 **Recorder:** record final decisions of the group regarding placement on the continuum;

3 **Time Monitor:** attend to the time allotted for the activity, alerting the discussion leader when the discussion gets bogged down; and

4 **Language Monitor:** make sure the group members are polite and respectful and use art vocabulary when appropriate.

After this activity, the teacher led the entire class in a discussion, asking the small groups to report on their decisions. She then suggested that students use their "Thoughts About Art" journals to record their own personal reflections about the ideas of art and beauty. She also urged them to list their own questions about art and beauty, telling them that they should refer to these questions throughout the unit.

*This unit was designed by Michelle Mattoon of Mitchell Elementary School, Plano, Texas.

Promoting Student Reflection

With the goal of helping students to become active, independent, and self-regulating learners, we need to assist them in becoming aware of how they learn best. They need to be aware of their own learning styles and what factors help or impede their learning. Accordingly, teachers can assist them in being reflective about what they have learned, how they have learned, and what they hope to do in the future as active learners. This can be done orally and informally, as the teacher functions as coach during student investigations, or in writing and in a more formal way. For example, art teachers have long known the benefits of having students keep sketchbooks. The sketchbook can be a valuable place for students not only to record their visual records but also to reflect in writing about their ideas and work in progress. The teacher presents prompts for students to consider as they reflect on their ideas and learning.

Teachers have developed many specific strategies to assist students in their learning. Role-playing, concept maps, game-like activities, and the use of worksheets and handouts are a few of the strategies teachers routinely use to move students toward a deeper understanding of important ideas. We have not described such strategies in depth but have suggested that curriculum planners select or design their own strategies that will engage students in substantive ways. The Curriculum Guidelines for the TETAC project contained a list of considerations for planning instruction. We include these here with the hope that they might assist curriculum planners in this important part of the planning process.

A Check on Content and Instruction

The following questions included in the original TETAC Curriculum Guidelines proved helpful to TETAC teachers as they planned their units of study.

1 Are all four disciplines—artmaking, art criticism, art history, aesthetics—appropriately developed with enduring ideas about the arts, relevant knowledge, and skills?

2 Does the unit address sufficiently all the knowledge and skills that need to be taught in order for students to achieve the unit goals and objectives?

3 Does the unit address knowledge and skills in logical sequence?

4 When concepts/key terms are introduced, are they sufficiently developed?

5 Do the enduring ideas, key concepts, and essential questions provide focus and cohesiveness throughout the unit?

6 Are the concepts and skills appropriate for student development levels?

7 Are substantive connections between art and other content areas developed as appropriate?

8 Are the necessary resources/background materials for teaching the unit listed?

9 Do activities and questions provide substantive engagement for students?

10 Are connections to prior knowledge and skills and real-life situations provided?

11 Are there assessment expectations for students?

12 Are opportunities provided for practice of new skills and concepts?

13 Are there opportunities for students to ask questions?

14 Are there opportunities for student-directed discussion?

15 Are a variety of learning activities provided that allow students to make individual and collaborative substantive contributions to the group effort?

16 Are opportunities provided for student self-reflection and metacognition?

17 Are opportunities provided for critical thinking?

18 Is there an audience beyond the teacher for student work and responses?

19 Are materials appropriate for student developmental levels?

Source: The National Arts Education Consortium, "Goals and Expectations for the Transforming Education Through the Arts Challenge," February 26, 1999.

Notes

1 D. M. Ogle. "K-W-L: A teaching model that develops active reading of informational text," *The Reading Teacher* 39 (1986), pp. 564–70.

2 E. S. Ellis, L. A. Worthington. Research Synthesis on Effective Teaching Principles and the Design of Quality Tools for Educators 1994, NCITE (National Center to Improve the Tools of Educators, University of Oregon) Technical Publication, Tech. Rep. No. 5, (1994), p. 38 (idea.uoregon.edu/~ncite/documents/techrep/tech05.pdf).

3 Ibid., p. 38.

Chapter

6

Targeting Understanding:

Assessment and the Curriculum

"That is what learning is. You suddenly understand something you've understood all your life, but in a new way. "
—Doris Lessing

Upper-elementary students at Wallace Smith Elementary School in Ooltewah, Tennessee, created a time capsule to be opened in two hundred years. Among the many items placed inside were the names of two works of art, one in the visual arts and one in music, that the students believed best reflected their world at the time. The selection of these two works was part of an end-of-unit performance task. The task was designed to provide students with the opportunity to demonstrate their understanding of the ideas and concepts investigated in an interdisciplinary unit entitled "The Blues: Sing It or See It?"

6.1 Romare Bearden, Empress of the Blues, 1974. Collage, 36" x 48". Smithsonian American Art Museum, Washington, DC/Art Resource, NY.

This unit was grounded in two related enduring ideas, "The arts reflect the history and culture of people" and "The arts mirror multiple viewpoints on a subject or event." During the course of the unit, the students learned much about the blues. They listened to several pieces of music and discussed them among themselves and with their teacher, who provided them with information about the time and culture in which the works were created. They wrote about the kinds of dilemmas that they face in their own lives and composed blues verses of their own. This unit of study also introduced them to the works of Romare Bearden, a collage artist who once said that for him, making a collage was like making music. They considered this idea as they created collages based on their own versions of the blues. The focus throughout the

unit was on the way in which blues artists and visual artists such as Bearden create their art by tapping into the struggles and events of ordinary life in their time. In doing so, artists will often address similar subjects or events from very different perspectives.

Prior to making their selections for the time capsule, the students worked with their teacher to create a set of criteria. These criteria guided small groups in selecting the two artworks that they then proposed to the class, along with their carefully constructed reasons. The entire class decided which two works would be included in the classroom time capsule. In creating criteria, selecting specific artworks, proposing these to the large group, and, finally, in judging those works that best met the criteria, the students were involved in complex cognitive work. As they

Chapter 6

offered well-supported explanations, interpretations, and judgments, the students applied their newly constructed knowledge and understanding to a real-world situation—that of adding to a class time capsule. In the process, their teacher was able to determine the extent to which her class understood the enduring ideas and key concepts of the unit. Additionally, she was able to observe the extent to which they used critical thinking skills so important to a comprehensive approach to the study of art.

Dixie Eiseman, the teacher who created this unit, stated, "The use of a problem-based learning scenario furnishes the students with a viable tool for conveying what they understand about the blues and about multiple ways of conveying the blues. The creation of their own rubric will also demonstrate their understanding of the enduring ideas reflected in this unit."

Assessment Is Integral to Planning

For Ms. Eiseman and other teachers who identify the enduring ideas to be explored in a unit and specific objectives related to particular subject areas, assessment can and should be an integral part of planning. Once we identify the understanding, knowledge, and skills that we believe are important for students to learn, we need to consider the ways in which they will demonstrate their learning. As discussed in the previous chapter, we design instructional strategies that will assist students in meeting these goals. One of the main purposes of assessment is to evaluate and improve student learning. Obviously, if we discover that students fail to understand or to use their new knowledge or skills appropriately, we make decisions about what to do next, and reflect upon what we might have done better. Another purpose of assessment is to further improve our instructional practice.

While planning for her students' understanding of the enduring ideas and key concepts of the lesson,

**End-of-Unit Performance Task:
Creating a Picture Book**

In a fifth-grade unit entitled "Thriving on Affection: The Enduring Love Affair Between People and Their Pets," the students explored a range of artworks that exemplified the enduring idea "artists express interpretations of human emotion in artworks and they often include pet animals as representative of bonds of affection."* The end-of-unit task was to draw upon personal experiences with pets and pet ownership to develop a picture book for their kindergarten reading partners. The students used disposable cameras to capture their own images of the affectionate bond between humans and pets and, in so doing, demonstrated their understanding of the ideas and concepts central to the unit.

*This unit was designed by Kelly Smith, Oakhurst Elementary School, Fort Worth, Texas.

Ms. Eiseman also taught the unit with further specific objectives in mind. Her written unit plan included reference to several standards in music, visual arts, language arts, and social studies. Each lesson contained plans to assess student learning relative to these objectives. For example, to assess the extent to which students were able to identify distinguishing characteristics of making music and making a collage, she had the students create Venn diagrams comparing the two processes. To assess how well students understood and were able to use the AAB form of blues writing, she checked their blues verses. Curriculum planning always involves consideration of the ways in which students will be able to demonstrate the understanding, knowledge, and skills we have deemed important.

The example of the time capsule as an end-of-unit performance task highlights an important notion presented in this book—that a unit can be planned around an enduring idea that is important for students to understand and that specific knowledge and skills can also be addressed within such a unit. The understanding of the enduring idea is what we hope students will carry with them into adulthood. The specific knowledge and skills related to a topic such as the blues in music and art are dynamically contextualized within the unit and provide the means for constructing understanding of the enduring ideas. Finally, and what is significant in terms of the focus of this chapter, assessment tasks provide opportunities for students to demonstrate their knowledge, skills, and understanding.

Assessment Is Natural to Teaching

As teachers conduct their classes, they routinely check to determine how well students are doing, what they seem to grasp, and what needs to be addressed in an alternative way. Teachers use a variety of strategies for gathering such information. They observe student behavior, ask questions, listen to student responses, consider student works-in-progress, and so on. This kind of assessment is informal and formative—informal because it is quick and spontaneous; formative because it serves as a means of assessing student learning during the course of instruction within a unit of study and it is not tied to specific means for reporting out information. The purpose is diagnostic; the teacher and students are able to discern what they have learned relative to the unit and lesson objectives and to make improvements midstream.

Because teachers want their students to learn, they often employ intuitive means for determining how things are going. Intuition is important and is often the starting point for good teaching and, in particular, appropriate assessment. To take advantage of the potential of assessment to improve teaching and learning, however, what teachers do naturally should become more deliberate, systematic, and purposeful.

The Importance of Alignment

When curriculum planning involves identifying enduring ideas and key concepts that guide the planning of instruction, and when these ideas and concepts consistently ground teaching decisions throughout the unit, then one would assume that the teacher will focus assessment on these important aspects of the unit. Accordingly, when planners take seriously the importance of process skills related to disciplined inquiry, and when instruction includes emphasis on these skills, one would assume that the teacher will look to student progress relative to these important processes in the course of teaching the unit. Consistent attention in instruction to the important ideas, concepts, and skills to be learned is the first step to becoming more systematic about formative assessment.

Checking for Understanding

Formative assessment can be fairly simple. For example, after engaging kindergarten and first-grade students in a discussion of Mary Cassatt's painting *Young Mother Sewing,* the teacher asked, "What are the most important things we have learned about the artwork?"* The teacher then distributed photocopies of the artwork to each child, explaining that they were to take them home to share with their families. In addition, she asked the students to write a note to their family members sharing with them what they had learned about the artwork and its meaning. These notes provided the teacher with additional information for formative assessment.

*This unit was designed by Barbara McHaffie, Kate Sullivan Elementary School, Tallahassee, Florida.

6.2 Moving from student to student to talk about work in progress, teachers informally assess students' apparent understanding of the concepts of the unit as well as their process skills.

Formative and Summative Assessment

Charting Responses

In the first lesson of a primary-level unit entitled "It's a Small World: Celebrations," the teacher distributed postcards of various celebrations and had students discuss their thoughts about the following questions: Why do people celebrate? Why do we celebrate certain events and not others? What do people do when they celebrate? What is a celebration? As students responded with their ideas, the teacher recorded them on a large chart, making a point to place student initials next to each response. The completed chart, with the student initials, assisted the teacher in assessing student ability to engage in large-group discussions, one of the objectives of the lesson.

Mini Portfolios

In the same unit, the teacher had students store their work in a mini portfolio. Toward the end of the unit, she reviewed the objectives of the unit and the rubric to be used for assessment. She provided students with the opportunity to select from their work those items that they believed best showed their understanding of the concepts and skills addressed by the unit.*

*This unit was designed by Kellie K. Joy, Clinton Elementary School, Lincoln Public Schools, Lincoln, Nebraska.

We found that assessment of important targeted learning is not as easily incorporated into curriculum planning as we would hope. Many art teachers with whom we worked learned to identify the enduring ideas, key concepts, and important skills in the early stages of planning, but then initially assessed tangential rather than the essential ideas, concepts, and skills put forward in their plans. For example, in some cases in the early stages of the TETAC project, art teachers tended to focus attention only upon completed student artwork, rather than other products or behaviors, when they assessed student learning. In addition, art teachers often looked for only "creativity" or "originality" in student work when they had not identified creativity and originality as important outcomes for the unit. Similarly, we found that teachers tended to single out student "effort" when they had not included an emphasis on effort in their unit or lesson objectives.

There are a few factors at work in this seeming disconnect between what curriculum planners identify as important learning and what they ultimately assess. First of all, there is a long tradition in art education of focusing only on student art products, both in instruction and assessment, even when claiming that deep understanding of ideas and concepts is an important goal. Another factor may well be related to deeply embedded beliefs about art and art teaching. In the examples above, a holdover from thought that creativity and originality are paramount in artmaking, and deeply held convictions against grading student art probably account for the inconsistency between objectives and assessment. A final factor that might be at work is a tendency to separate, rather than align, objectives, instruction, and assessment in the process of planning a unit.

Alignment of objectives, instruction, and assessment simply means that once we identify the enduring ideas, key concepts, and important skills we want students to learn in a unit of study, we then teach toward this learning, and we look for evidence of this learning through assessment. As noted, we look for this evidence during the course of teaching the unit, for diagnostic purposes, in the form of formative assessment, but we also do this in the form of summative assessment. Summative assessment differs from formative assessment in that it generally takes place after a period of instruction and the teacher makes judgments about a student's achievement at this specific point in time. From the students' perspective, such assessment provides an opportunity for them to demonstrate what they have learned. Another purpose of summative assessment is to collect information for reporting student achievement. This often includes assigning a grade and communicating achievement to students, parents, future teachers, and the community. Whether for formative or summative assessment purposes, however, it is crucial to assess what we have deemed, in the early stages of planning, as important student learning.

New Targets for Assessment

In Chapter 5, we emphasized the need for curriculum planners to design instructional strategies that will engage learners, activate their questions, prompt investigation, and assist them in constructing new knowledge and understandings. We called for a classroom environment that values the student as inquirer, researcher, and problem solver; that values the need for students to be self-determined and to feel capable and comfortable in applying their skills to construct new knowledge. We discussed the importance of providing opportunities for students to engage in critical thinking as they apply their knowledge in real-world or relevant situations. In a comprehensive approach to the study of art—the approach we have endorsed

Summative Assessment

Summative assessment "is used at the end of a course or segment of learning, for the purpose of summarizing what students know and are able to do, and in conjunction with set task dimensions, criteria, and scoring strategies."* Summative assessments vary from paper-and-pencil tests to a wide range of performance tasks.

*Donna Kay Beattie, *Assessment in Art Education* (Worcester, MA: Davis Publications, 1997), p. 84.

6.3 Students take pride in their developing skills in artmaking. In planning, it is important to allot time for students to practice such skills.

6.4 *As teachers seek ways to assess for deep understanding, they often consider student artwork along with students' reflections about their work and how it connects with the enduring ideas and key concepts of the unit.*

throughout this book—students are engaged in inquiry associated with art criticism, art history, aesthetics, and artmaking in order to develop deep understandings of enduring ideas and key concepts. To embrace this approach to the study of art is to recognize that assessment must address the extent to which students have constructed new understandings relative to the enduring ideas and key concepts, and also the extent to which they have appropriately used process skills associated with the disciplines. In other words, as we shift in our conceptions of learning, curriculum content, and appropriate, important classroom behaviors, we need to shift in our conception of what is to be assessed and the best means for assessing it.

The Importance of Criteria

How will students demonstrate their deep and complex understandings? How will they demonstrate their ability to engage in inquiry associated with the disciplines? These are the questions that guide the planning of assessment. Generally, this means that students will need to have opportunities to perform in ways that they can apply their new understanding and use their inquiry skills. One important way in which such opportunities can be provided is through what are called performance tasks. With shifts in our conceptions of learning, curriculum content, and classroom behaviors, we find that we need to design more performance tasks as part of curriculum planning.

From working with the teachers in the TETAC project, we found that teachers actually enjoy the process of creating performance tasks. As with designing engaging instructional activities, teachers imagine a wide range of scenarios and problems through which students can demonstrate their knowledge. What is crucial, however, but what is often left out, are the criteria to be used in the assessment of learning. In addition to creating interesting and engaging tasks, teachers need to consider what would be a successful completion of the task. Given the goals of the unit, what should teachers look for? What should students aim for?

Criteria are important, first of all, for the purpose of clarity. Especially when performance tasks are highly engaging, it is easy to forget (or ignore) the purpose of the task. When we carefully consider the criteria, we clarify what is really important—what is valued in student work and behavior.

When students are clear about what is expected of them, what they are to address in their performance, they are more likely to engage in self-evaluation and reflection. By attending to the criteria, students tend to focus on what is important, and accordingly their learning is enhanced. Assessment is often thought of as a means to help students learn what we intend them to learn, but it is actually the awareness of the criteria, not engagement in the task itself, that promotes such learning.

Since criteria play such a significant role, curriculum planners must make sure to include them when designing and implementing performance tasks. Moreover, it is imperative that the criteria are the right criteria for the task—appropriate in terms of what the students are to do and what learning they are to demonstrate in their performance. Criteria must be central, not tangential, to what we have deemed as important learning.

Transparency

A shift in our conception of assessment also suggests that we not think of assessment as something done to students. If students are to be active, involved learners, then they also need to be aware of where they are going and how they are progressing toward that end. In the past, it was not uncommon for teachers to surprise students with tests or quizzes. In the case of studio art, students who thought about the grade they might "receive" for a project wondered what the teacher was "looking for." When we think about this now, especially in light of our new understanding of what it means to construct knowledge, it seems silly. Not only should students be aware of criteria for successful completion of a task, they ought to be involved whenever possible in the development of criteria. In the time capsule example described at the beginning of this chapter, the students collaborated with the teacher to develop appropriate criteria for the selection of the artworks for the capsule. In doing so, they needed to bring to the experience what they had learned was important, along with their recognition of the enduring ideas and key concepts of the unit of study.

Clarifying What Is Important

One of the rewarding features of designing good assessment is that, in the process, we are forced to examine our assumptions about curriculum content and desired student behaviors as we single out what is really important for students to learn. For example, many art teachers believe it is important for students to know the elements and principles of design. In designing assessment, a teacher would need to consider what students would do to demonstrate this knowledge. One approach to this would be to require that students memorize definitions of the various elements and principles of design and provide these definitions orally or in writing.

But is being able to recall a memorized definition really what we believe is important in this case? Most would agree that it is much more important that students be able to employ the elements and principles of design to express ideas in their artworks, or

High School Assessment with Criteria

In the following example, lesson objectives for studio production are tied to the enduring idea and goals for the unit. Students are provided with criteria in the form of a rubric prior to engaging in the tasks.*

Unit Title: Cultural Influence

Enduring Idea: Our culture and personal experiences make us who we are.

Unit Goals:

1 Students will understand that all people are influenced by cultural and personal experiences.

2 Students will become aware that they also are influenced by their cultural and personal experiences and can express that in a personal artwork.

*This unit was designed by Janet Parker, Woodland High School, Woodland, California.

Art Production Objectives:

1 Students will be able to create a visual image that communicates an important cultural event from their lives and explain the event through a written vignette.

2 Students will be able to employ stylistic characteristics of Carmen Lomas Garza—the use of bright colors and one-dimensional figures.

Students complete their paintings and vignettes and then write about what they have done, discussing the following:

• What personal experience did you show in your artwork?

• How did you communicate your culture through your artwork?

• Compare and contrast your artwork and writing with Garza's or Cisneros's work. What are the similarities and differences in the two works? Remember to refer to specific elements in your work to support your ideas.

Assignment: Art Production and Reflection	Excellent	Good	Needs Work
Personal Experience in Artwork	Artwork clearly displays a personal experience within the context of own culture.	Artwork somewhat displays a personal experience and somewhat references culture.	Slight or no reference to personal experience and culture.
Culture in Artwork explained	Culture represented in artwork is discussed with clear evidence and details.	Culture is discussed adequately with some evidence.	The writer does not discuss connection with his/her culture.
Compares/Contrasts artwork to Garza or Cisneros	The writer deeply explores the connection between the artwork and the work of Garza or Cisneros through comparing and contrasting.	The writer somewhat presents concrete connections between the two works of art.	The writer fails to adequately explore the connections between the two pieces of art.

that they be able to identify ways in which elements and principles help to convey meaning in artworks made by others. In designing assessment, we have the opportunity to shift priorities, which often means that we should reconsider what we have long thought to be important for students to learn.

We could go on with these kinds of examples. For instance, is neatness in artworks really important? One might imagine any number of instances when it would be important, but it is also feasible that an artwork can be powerful and not be tidy or neat. In the time capsule example, as students provide reasons for their selected artworks, would *any* reason count as appropriate or would reasons associated with the enduring ideas of the unit be more important? When identifying criteria for successful performance, teachers are confronted with decisions such as these.

Assessing What Is Important

Once we identify what we believe is important to assess, we need to create an assessment that will actually address this. We have emphasized the importance of aiming for understanding of enduring ideas and key concepts. We have said that understanding is complex; to say that a student understands something is to say that the student has a certain degree of sophistication relative to a concept or topic. This sophistication can be demonstrated when students do such things as offer explanations, make generalizations, provide examples, apply what they know to new situations, make comparisons, formulate and answer questions, make judgments about quality, synthesize information, and represent a topic or idea in a new way. In order to provide opportunities for students to perform in ways that demonstrate understanding, we must provide opportunities for students to engage in the kind of cognitive work mentioned here. It should be clear that no one kind of activity

Evidence of Understanding

The TETAC faculty at Ohio State University created the following list of skills that provide evidence of understanding, along with sample ways to describe desired responses.

Skills for Understanding

- Organizes knowledge
- Analyzes processes
- Constructs interpretations
- Makes connections
- Makes comparisons
- Translates knowledge into symbolic form
- Makes predictions
- Summarizes knowledge
- Makes inferences
- Formulates judgments
- Links the specific with the general
- Considers implications
- Finds examples
- Engages contrast
- Experiments, tests
- Identifies significant information
- Raises questions

Descriptors

- **Explanations/interpretations**
  Fully supported, compelling, deep, broad, reasoned, illuminating, perceptive, insightful, convincing, multidimensional, inventive

- **Visual, verbal, and kinesthetic expressions**
  Inventive, focused, insightful, powerful, unpredictable, authentic, persuasive, purposeful, subtle, elaborated, imaginative, fully developed, finely honed, layered in meaning

- **Application to new cases**
  Perceptive, insightful, appropriate, fluid, considered, original, authentic, comprehensive

Source: The Ohio State University TETAC faculty, unpublished presentation notes.

will suffice in this regard. A single task such as recalling a definition, for example, cannot provide evidence of complex understanding. Assessment must be multidimensional in order to provide a rich portrayal of student learning.

We have also proposed that the methods associated with art-historical inquiry, art criticism, philosophical inquiry, and artmaking are dynamically connected to the development of deep understandings. In Chapter 4 we discussed the kinds of process skills associated with these areas of inquiry. In instruction, and therefore in assessment, we can also target these skills. Here again, we need to make certain that the assessment actually assesses what we intend it to assess. Using the earlier example, if we want to assess students' ability to use the elements and principles of design to convey ideas in their own artworks, then we need to create a task that will allow them to do so. In this case, a task that requires students to view a work of art created by someone else and to analyze the way the artist has employed the elements and principles of design to convey meaning would be inappropriate. This task could be used to assess student ability to analyze the formal components of an artwork, but it would not assist us in determining the extent to which students are able to use these formal components to convey ideas in their own artworks. Similarly, if we want to assess students' ability to construct plausible interpretations of artworks, we would not provide students with a task that requires them to recall something they have read or memorized. Instead, we would, provide them with an opportunity to look carefully at the components of an artwork, noting symbols and other meaning-laden aspects of the work, and make connections with what they know and what they see to address questions such as, "What is this artwork about? What is its meaning or message?" We would require that students provide

reasons for their interpretation and that their reasons be grounded in the artwork and in related contextual information.

Assessment: An Instrument of Learning

Many strategies used in the instruction of concepts and skills can also be used to assess the extent to which students have learned them. For example, small-group discussions about an artwork or an issue can be used to help students deepen their understanding about a particular artwork or type of artwork or issue and to assist them in developing skills of rational discussion. Small-group discussion can also be used to assess the extent to which students can do these things. Observation would be used, perhaps with a checklist in which the teacher notes whether comments made or questions raised by individual students indicate understanding of the issues and/or their ability to engage in rational discussion.

Worksheets completed by students following a discussion can help students reflect on the issues as well as demonstrate their comprehension of the issues and factors involved. Engagement in studio work that requires students to employ concepts and skills for the purposes of expression can also be used to assess the extent to which students grasp these issues. Group projects, individual journal or sketchbook entries, individual artworks, essays, worksheets—all part of the instruction—can also be used to assess student learning.

These approaches are tied to the notion that assessment can serve as an instrument of learning. We help move students to new understandings because the tasks we identify isolate those things upon which it is important to focus. The same guidelines for designing instruction are used for designing assessment. The activity should be engaging, involving students in inquiry and the application of knowledge.

When teachers and students recognize the potential for instructional strategies to reveal important information about students' understanding and skill, they come to think of assessment as ongoing, an integral part of the classroom experience.

Teacher, Peer, and Self-Assessment

Most of the assessment that takes place in the classroom is teacher-directed, but students can also take an active role. In a classroom environment in which students are aware of the enduring ideas and key concepts of the unit, recognize the importance of developing understanding of these ideas and concepts, and know that their ideas and questions are valued, working together toward understanding the goals of the unit becomes everyone's responsibility. Ongoing assessment of progress toward these ends is not seen as the sole responsibility of the teacher. Rather, students engage in self-assessment and are often called upon to engage in assessment of the progress of their peers. The teacher provides opportu-

6.5 Rubrics were shared with students early in the unit and in some cases were created by both teachers and students.

Rubric for Interpreting Artworks

The following is a generic holistic rubric that can be used to assess middle school students' interpretations of artworks. A student should be able to construct an interpretation of an artwork's main idea, or what the artwork is about. The interpretation should be supported with well-selected details from the artwork (subject matter, visual elements, organization, use of media) and with relevant contextual information (including their own experiences and points of view).

4 The student work shows an insightful, illuminating, and interesting interpretation of an artwork, fully supported by evidence, including a thoughtful analysis of subject matter, visual elements, organization, and use of media. The student is able to integrate relevant contextual information that strongly connects to the interpretation.

3 The student work shows a plausible interpretation of an artwork, adequately supported by a number of examples and details. The student is able to refer to relevant contextual information and provide a satisfactory connection to the interpretation.

2 The student work shows a simple interpretation, minimally supported with references to some details in the artwork. The student can provide some contextual information but does not relate it to the meaning of the artwork.

1 The student work does not address the meaning or message of the artwork, or it begins to do so, but then turns to other ideas or topics. When details of the work are mentioned, they are not offered in support of an interpretation. The student provides little or no contextual information related to the meaning of the artwork.

Source: Eldon Katter and Marilyn Stewart, *Art: A Personal Journey Teacher's Resource Binder* (Worcester, MA: Davis Publications, 2002), p. 19.

Using a Template for an End-of-Unit Performance Task

In a sixth-grade unit entitled "A Monument and Monumental Sculpture's Role in Its Geographic Site," student activities centered around the enduring idea and key concepts of the purposes and roles of monuments and monumental sculptures in their geographic sites.* As a result of their investigations, students were "to be able to recognize the historical significance of a monument, understand the monument's place in our present society, and how its existence might influence the future." To demonstrate their understanding, students were provided with the following end-of-unit performance task.

Goal: Your task is to design a brochure that will advertise a specific monument or monumental sculpture. This brochure will highlight the historical significance of the monument, communicate an understanding of the monument's place in our present society, and how the monument's existence might influence the future.

Role: You are an artist in an advertising agency and have been asked to create a brochure to advertise a monument or monumental sculpture. Your job is to increase tourism to this sight.

*This unit was designed by Deborah Bowers Kippley, Tara Heights Elementary School, Papillion, Nebraska

Audience: Your audience is the general public—anyone who would be a potential visitor to the monument or monumental sculpture.

Situation: A group of people living near the monument or monumental sculpture you have selected is looking to raise tourism. Your agency has been employed to create a brochure to entice people to visit this site for its historical significance, to demonstrate the monument's place in our present society, and to highlight how the monument's existence might influence the future. The brochure should include images and descriptions of the site.

Production or Performance: You will create a trifold brochure that communicates the important features of the monument and includes at least three images from three different views.

Standards for Success: The student has successfully completed this activity if she/he has created a trifold brochure, including references to the historical significance of the monument, reference to the monument's place in our present society, and how the monument's existence might influence the future. The three views of the monument may be digital, drawn, or cut from a magazine. The visual and written information should hook the audience and convince people of the importance of visiting the site.

nities for self- and peer assessment, relying upon an established environment of inquiry that allows for such assessment to flow naturally in the course of the unit.

Strategies for self-assessment can be as simple as asking students to select their best work to meet specific criteria or to use their journal or sketchbook to reflect upon what they have learned by addressing prompts provided by the teacher. Peer assessment, too, can be as simple as having students work in pairs, exchange their work, and comment upon it relative to a set of criteria. As any teacher knows, peer assessment can be risky, given the social development of some students. It takes time and sensitivity to create an environment of mutual respect in which peer assessment can easily take place. However, because students do care and respond to what their peers have to say about their work in progress it is worth attempting when the teacher believes students are ready for it.

A Checklist for Assessment Planning

There are times in which it makes sense to design strategies specifically for the purpose of assessing student understanding or skill proficiency. We offer the following steps, recognizing that the process of designing assessment strategies rarely is linear and that teachers often begin the process in different ways, entering the process at various points. We also recommend that teachers consider sharing the development of performance tasks and criteria with students, in which case the same process would be employed.

1 Identify the purpose of the assessment.

   a Will you use the assessment to determine what your students know and are able to do in order to begin the unit of study?

   b Will you use the assessment to determine how things are going; what students have learned in the process of the unit thus far?

   c Will you use the assessment as an end-of-unit demonstration of learning?

2 Clarify what it is that you wish to assess.

   a Do you wish to assess understanding of enduring ideas and key concepts?

   b Do you wish to assess process skills related to disciplined inquiry?

   c Do you wish to assess both understanding and process skills?

3 Brainstorm ideas for possible ways in which students can demonstrate learning.

   a What instructional or assessment strategies have engaged students in the past? Can these be adapted for your purposes?

   b What new scenarios or problems can you think of that would allow students to apply what they understand or are able to do?

6.6 In the unit for which this artwork was created, not only did students develop models for monuments and memorials, but they also engaged in research about a social cause, wrote about why the cause is important, developed a prospectus for a memorial or monument to the cause, and created blueprints for their structures. Teachers who wish to gain a rich portrait of student learning will look to multiple sources such as these.

c What products might students create in order to demonstrate what they understand or are able to do? Will students construct an interpretation, create a visual product of some sort, provide an oral performance, construct a written response to a series of prompts, write a journal reflection, etc?

4 Select from your brainstorming list those strategies, problems, and/or products that will best serve to elicit understanding and/or skills that you wish to assess. As you consider a performance task, ask yourself the following:

a Does it appropriately relate to the enduring idea and key concepts of the unit?

b Will students be required to use process skills associated with disciplined inquiry?

c Is the performance task authentic, relating to real-world situations that hold interest for the students?

d Is the task complex enough for students to engage in it in a variety of ways to demonstrate their understanding and skill? Are there multiple dimensions to the task?

e Will the task allow for active participation on the part of students?

f Is the task feasible? Can it be accomplished in a reasonable amount of time? Are required materials and resources available?

6.7 In an environment in which learning is everyone's responsibility, students can freely talk with each other about their work and assist each other in meeting the unit objectives.

g Will all of your students be able to engage in this task?

5 Determine criteria for assessment.

a What will count as a successful completion of the performance task?

b What should all performances contain in order to demonstrate understanding and/or targeted skills?

c What might performances contain that will be tangential to the targeted understanding and skills?

6 Based upon consideration of #5, create a rubric, in which you delineate levels of achievement, to be shared with students and used in evaluation of the performance task.

a Given what will count as a successful completion of the performance task, what might count as a partial completion?

b What will count as an advanced completion?

c What will count as minimal completion of the task?

7 If advisable, given administrative requirements of your teaching situation, assign a numerical scale for your rubric, assigning a point number for the levels of achievement identified in #6 above.

8 Make sure that the task parameters, criteria, and levels of achievement are clear to the students prior to their engagement with the performance.

9 Use the performance task with students. Evaluate its effectiveness and make alterations as needed for the future.

We recommend that those seeking further information, along with additional examples of various types of assessment, refer to Donna Kay Beattie's *Assessment in Art Education,* in this same Art Education in Practice series.

Art and Integrated Curriculum

"We are currently witnessing a renewed interest in integrated curriculum. Simultaneously, I believe that the art world and our general modes of communication have also changed in such a way as to make art potentially more central to the curriculum."

—Art educator Michael Parsons[1]

Because the TETAC project was conceived to link the arts to other areas of the school curriculum and "demonstrate the value of the arts as part of the core curriculum," a consideration of integrated curriculum became essential.[2] The roots of interest in integrated curriculum extend to the early part of the twentieth century with John Dewey and Progressive education.[3] Kathy Lake enumerates a host of positive reasons often cited for integrating the curriculum. These include the knowledge explosion, the increase in state mandates to education, concerns with educational relevancy, and the promotion of holistic learning by cognitive theorists and brain researchers.[4] Why should art curriculum and instruction engage with integrated curriculum? We consider this question from the perspective of how curriculum integration benefits art learning and from the alternate viewpoint of what art learning brings to other subject areas.

Looking Back

"The belief that all genuine education comes about through experience does not mean that all experiences are genuinely or equally educative."

—John Dewey

J. Dewey, *Experience & Education* (New York: Touchstone, 1938), p. 25.

7.1 *Teacher planning time is essential for integrated curriculum work.*

At the most practical level, integrated curriculum involves decisions about how many school subjects will be linked and for what length of time, how teacher planning will occur, and how the school schedule will be affected. Such issues matter considerably, and often the practical becomes the proverbial stumbling block. This is something we learned through the TETAC project, as common planning time for teachers, school schedules, and state and district mandates became contentious items seriously thwarting curriculum integration. While realizing the decided impact of the practical, it is the more conceptual aspects of curriculum integration that concerns us in this chapter.

Art educator Judith Burton observes, concerning art and integrated curriculum, that there exists a distinction between learning "in" and learning "through" art and artistry.[6] She insightfully recognizes that both approaches, learning *in* art and learning *through* art, are necessary when integrating art curriculum, but we should be aware that "underachievement in learning in art has direct consequences for learning though art."[7] That is, if one does not possess the requisite understandings of art itself, the ability to link art to other areas will definitely be impeded. This represents strong support for engaging students with art learning in a rigorous and focused manner. For this reason, in Chapter 4, "Making Choices: Selecting Lesson Content to Build on Unit Foundations," we presented art content as a conceptual structure composed of key art understandings and inquiry concepts and principles, not as lists of artworks, artists, styles, time periods, and art media to be studied.

In what manner does integrated curriculum enhance, serve, and benefit art learning? In the following pages, we examine why the instruction of enduring ideas and contemporary art improves if they are linked to other school subject knowledge.

Checklist

- *How valuable is the organizing central idea for students to think about and assimilate into their way of looking at the world . . . ?*

This is the purpose of writing a rationale explaining why a particular enduring idea is worth teaching to a specific population of students.

- *To what degree might students learn the concepts better than if they had been taught separately . . . ?*

This question probes the heart of integrated curriculum. Asking such a question should reveal meaningful connections between subject areas and create a fertile context for shaping the integrated unit in more productive ways. Asking this question can help prevent teachers from thinking of integrated curriculum only from the perspective of their own subject area.

- *How much time is available for communication among teachers during common planning or teaching time . . . ?*

The lack of adequate planning time or common planning time is one of the major stumbling blocks to successful integrated curriculum, particularly in the elementary school. Often elementary school schedules do not permit arts teachers to plan with classroom teachers. This is a problem, since joint teacher planning is essential to integrated curriculum.

Focused planning time is basic to integrated curriculum, and meeting at the photocopier or in the hallway is not sufficient. As a unit is being taught, ongoing planning is necessary, since adjustments and changes to instruction are always a part of good teaching.

- *In what ways can scheduling support interdisciplinary learning?*

Scheduling can often help or hinder in carrying forth an integrated curriculum unit. For instance, the art teacher must have contact with all the same students as other subject area teachers, that is, if some students are scheduled for one class but not another, integrated curriculum will be difficult. On the other hand, if classes in different subject areas are scheduled simultaneously this could allow for greater integration of learning, team teaching, and greater flexibility in students' use of time.

- *What support from key individuals or groups is needed . . . ?*

In the TETAC project, having administrative support at the principal level was essential for successful curriculum integration. Without such support, teachers often can't manage common planning time, receive needed professional development, acquire necessary materials and resources, or persuade doubtful parents and faculty of the benefits of the approach. Support at the district level can also matter as well. Think of the influence standardized testing exercises at the school level. Recently, author Peter Sacks issued a powerful critique of the rage for standardized testing among American schools, boldly arguing that America is paying a high price for such testing. There is little doubt that the powerful focus on standardized testing has created tensions for many educators who seek worthwhile educational experiences for their students, rather than the less sophisticated and desirable goals of rote memorization and reproduction of knowledge. In the TETAC project, this tension was noticeable as teachers who desired to devote more instructional time to integrated curriculum units were torn by demands to "teach to the test." Thus, district support has import as the expectations and requirements at this level can have a direct effect on integrated curriculum.

Sources: Northwest Regional Educational Laboratory (NWREL) (http://www.nwrel.org/comm/glance.html). P. Sacks, *Standardized Minds: High Price of America's Testing Culture and What We Can Do to Challenge It* (Cambridge, MA: Perseus Publishers, 1999).

FAQs

Why Integrate the Curriculum?

In *Making Connections: Teaching and the Human Brain,* authors Renata and Geoffrey Caine relate integrated curriculum to the way the brain works physiologically.

"Integrated curriculum is an effective way to teach and learn because it corresponds with the way our brain works physiologically. Rather than separating knowledge into discrete partitions, the brain creates a complex web of information that recognizes patterns. Moreover, learning within a known context or experience helps the brain remember information more effectively . . . In fact, the physical structure of the brain changes as a result of experience, and it grows and develops more in an interactive environment . . . Integrating curriculum is a way to capitalize on these existing features of the human brain and work with, rather than counter to its natural function."*

*Renata Nummela Caine and Geoffrey Caine, *Making Connections: Teaching and the Human Brain* (Alexandria, VA: Association for Supervision and Curriculum Development, 1992), pp. 5, 27–28 (http://www.arche works.org/Education/ic_guide_p3.html).

Linking Art Instruction to Other Subjects

Shaping art learning around the study of enduring ideas is central to the construction of curriculum as we envision it in this text. The arts are a major repository of human values, beliefs, aspirations, occupations, and achievement. As such, arts learning has an inherent bond with enduring ideas. This natural connection can be fostered by an integrated curriculum approach.

For example, the art criticism unit from Chapter 4 that featured Kenneth Treister's *Holocaust Memorial* could not have been taught without reference to a historical period. This art unit, which focused on the enduring idea of human suffering and a memorial dedicated to the Holocaust, was intimately linked and interwoven with historical events and easily integrated other school subjects, such as history and literature.

Because enduring ideas represent content that exceeds a single school subject, it is important to reach beyond a single school subject to develop substantive instruction. In an ideal situation, a diverse, committed group of art teachers and teachers of other school subjects would focus on an agreed-upon enduring idea, common theme, or issue, and have abundant planning and instructional time to reach the instructional goals. Occasionally, this scenario occurs, but not often enough in the real world of practice.

Enduring Ideas, Contemporary Art, and Meaningful Integration

Meaningful integrated curriculum requires a focus, such as an enduring idea, theme, or issue. The importance of this connecting linkage cannot be overemphasized. Simply teaching a common topic with perspectives provided by various school subjects does not produce meaningful learning. Heidi Hayes Jacobs recognizes this as the potpourri problem. She observes: "Many units become a sampling of knowledge from each discipline. If the subject is Ancient Egypt, there will be a bit of history about Ancient Egypt, a bit of literature, a bit of the arts, and so forth. Hirsch (1987) and Bloom (1987) have criticized this approach for its lack of focus."[8]

The impetus for enduring ideas during the TETAC project was an attempt to avoid exactly what Jacobs describes. If school subjects in the project were to be linked, there needed to be a meaningful conceptual connection between them; otherwise students would simply be amassing information.

It would not be difficult to argue that contemporary art demands an interdisciplinary approach for understanding its content and practices. In the past several decades, artists have engaged in artmaking that is connected to the social and political realms. Whether in regard to issues of identity, women and social power, multiculturalism and representation, ecology, or an overwhelming commodification of art and society, artists have become engaged with the social and cultural conversations of our time.

Constructing understandings about contemporary art often depends upon knowledge that is outside the bounds of art. For instance, installation artist Mark Dion assumes the practices of an archaeologist to question socially constructed boundaries erected between artifacts and art. Environmental artist Mel Chin draws heavily upon science in *Revival Field* to investigate the prospects of hyperaccumulator plants and land reclamation, and draws upon American history in *Spirit* to question the ecological balance of the prairie lands. Performance and installation artist Eleanor Antin references the destruction of Pompeii to draw analogies to contemporary times.

Modern art styles such as Impressionism, Cubism, or any of the multiple stylistic "isms" that evolved in the early twentieth century were often, although not always, interpreted without referencing the social or historical context. The modernist period, in which a formalist emphasis on the art elements and principles reigned supreme, left deep impressions on art education theory and practice. As acknowledged by Olivia Gude, as well as other art educators, formalist approaches don't offer the needed conceptual understandings and strategies for either responding to or creating art in contemporary times. Gude notes a need to forge a "fit between art of the time, the art theory and criticism that supported and developed the art, and the exercises by which students [are] introduced to the field."[9]

Heeding Gude's advice, we recommend that today's art classrooms engage students with contemporary art and understanding the research practices that contemporary artists such as Dion, Chin, and Antin use to produce their artworks.

7.2 *A Nebraska integrated curriculum unit incorporated the work of Regionalist artist Grant Wood and of novelist Willa Cather to engage high school students with the enduring idea of identity.*

Lists

The following contemporary artists all cross knowledge boundaries as part of their artmaking practice.

- *Mel Chin*

  Chin's work derives from a strong cultural perspective and, at times, he enlists the active participation of experts from knowledge areas outside of art. In creating *Revival Field* (1990–1993), he developed a working relationship with the scientist Rufus Chaney, a heavy-metals expert in the Environmental Chemistry Laboratory at the USDA's Agricultural Research Service in Beltsville, Maryland. *Revival Field* began when Chin happened upon an article about hyperaccumulators—plants that selectively absorb heavy metals from toxic soils as they grow. He and Chaney created test plantings of hyperaccumulators on toxic landfills as an art project. Chin says the project relates to his interest in alchemy, transformative processes, and the mutable nature of materials.

- *Robert Irwin*

  Robert Irwin, now over seventy years of age, began his career as an abstract expressionist painter and developed into a leader of the West Coast Light and Space movement with site-specific installations. Late in his career, he was commissioned to design a large garden as part of the Getty Center in Los Angeles, a complex of buildings designed by architect Richard Meir. Irwin was familiar with working within a specific context but had never designed a garden. He bought a thousand dollars' worth of gardening books and cut out pictures of the plants he liked, sorting the pictures by the height, texture, leaf shape, and color indicated. He visited nurseries around the state and had to admit that many of his choices simply would not grow in California. Irwin eventually created an interesting garden, though it was fourteen years in the making.

- *Pepón Osorio*

  Osorio bases his extravagant installations in the Latino community where he lives. His own education as a social worker informs his work, and at times he consults with others to develop a knowledge base for his productions. For instance, in

Scene of the Crime (Whose Crime?) (1993), Osorio's desire for authenticity extended to working with two police detectives who investigate homicides. Much of Osorio's research for his installations is informal, based upon personal relationships and interviews, such as the over forty hours he spent interviewing and videotaping an imprisoned Latino father and his teenaged son for the installation *Badge of Honor* (1996).

- *Walton Ford*

  A study of painter Walton Ford could fruitfully be integrated with studies in biology and botany as well as art history. In a review of Ford's work, Martha Schwendener observes, "Walton Ford regularly offers a web of images and text exhuming whole realms of history: the history of natural science and zoology; exploration (and its attendant exploitation) and colonization; the history of images, artistic and otherwise; even the history of history . . . Ford collapses the past into the present, offering images that are both new and old—summoning an Audubon stiffness while consciously tweaking that convention—and mining subjects pertinent to contemporary environmentalism and geopolitics."*

- *Eleanor Antin*

  Eleanor Antin ties her performance, film, and installation pieces to the past which she recontextualizes within the present. In her work, she has frequently reinvented her identity through figures from the past such as "Eleanor Nightingale," in *The Angel of Mercy* (1977) and "Eleanora Antinova" as the black ballerina of Segei Diaghilev's Ballets Russes in *The Ballerina and the Poet* (1974) and *The Ballerina and the Bum* (1974). In a photographic series, *The Last Days of Pompei* (2001), Antin draws parallels between Rome as a great world power living in affluence while actually on the brink of annihilation and America today. In the series, she directs a host of actors depicting decadent, affluent citizens of Pompeii idling, luxuriating, posing, and lounging in the present-day affluent town of La Jolla, California.

*Martha Schwendener, "Walton Ford," *ArtForum*, January 2003 (http://www. findarticles.com/cfls/m0268/5_41/96223242/p1/ article.jhtml).

Up to this point, we have considered why arts learning is enriched by connections to other school subjects, but we might also contemplate what the arts can contribute to student learning. What can the study of art bring to other school subjects? We propose two qualities that, if not unique to the arts, are central to their practice—a concern with metaphorical meaning and a recognition of aesthetic dimensions of knowing.

Art and the Uses of Metaphorical Understanding

The arts do not have a monopoly on interpretation. Both science and mathematics, for instance, are based in interpretations of the world. However, as Arthur Efland contends, "it is in the arts where the experience, nature, and structure of metaphor becomes the principal object of study."[10] Efland stresses that the arts are the place where the construction of metaphor is the principal object of study. Artworks are to be understood not as literal facts but as embodiments of other meanings. He emphatically declares, "It is *only in the arts where the processes and products of the imagination are encountered and explored in full consciousness*—where they become objects of inquiry, unlike in the sciences where the metaphors that are used remain hidden."[11] Efland's point is well taken in accounting for what the arts can contribute to the school curriculum. Not only are the arts a rich resource of objects that speak of human existence, past and present, but they invite—indeed they demand—interpretation of the world in ways that other subject areas do not.

How important is metaphorical meaning to our lives? George Lakoff and Mark Johnson call metaphor "one of our most important tools for trying to understand what cannot be fully comprehended: our feelings, aesthetic experiences, moral practices, and spiritual awareness."[12] The import of Lakoff and

Artist Talk: Contrasting the Literal and the Metaphorical

Video artist Bill Viola speaks of the power of metaphor and "trying to break the stranglehold of literal representation." He explains that literal representation, which is part of his video work, "is the danger point of the optical medium. Once you give the image-making process over to optics, you're automatically bound to the representation of the content, literally, visually." Viola explores technical strategies such as slowing down the movement in a film to circumvent the literal and get to the invisible content.

He observes that "the real energy always comes from invisible things, and that's where I want my camera to be, capturing the register of feelings, not the optical view."

Viola has discovered that if you want viewers to understand something, you don't literally describe it for them, give them pictures of it; rather you try to give them *the experience*. He explains, "If you're going after the experience, you don't go after the literal description of the thing. If you want to put someone out in Death Valley, and we're in a room in New York City in some museum, you turn out the lights. You don't show pictures on the wall. You know what I mean? You do something viscerally, physically, perceptually that puts them in that state. You speak in the language of the experience itself, in the present tense. This is about Being, not appearances."

Source: Bill Viola Interviewed by John G. Hanhardt in *Going Forth by Day* (New York: The Solomon R. Guggenheim Foundation, 2002), p. 105.

Inside the Classroom

A Nebraska high school English teacher engaged her students with exploring their own identity through a Willa Cather novel and the paintings of Grant Wood. In reading the following description, keep in mind questions such as how different would the curriculum unit have been without the inclusion of the arts? What did Grant Wood's depictions of Midwestern life of the early twentieth century bring to the students' understanding of identity? Imagine if the high school English students had merely discussed what it might have been like to discover identity growing up as a pioneer youth in Nebraska and how living in a particular geographic locale and time period can influence perceptions of identity, as opposed to experiencing these ideas through visual and verbal imagery.

"What did you learn in school today?" "Oh, we talked about who we are." This high school student in Columbus, Nebraska, was taking part in a curriculum unit, "The Search for Identity," during which she and her classmates will investigate questions about how identity is formed. They will consider factors that contribute to who they are and what control they have over who and what they may become. A mushy softball unit without intellectual rigor? Not at all. During the unit, the students will study three Nebraska youths who searched for their identity as pioneers during the 1800s as portrayed in Willa Cather's novel *My Antonia;* and consider Midwestern identity in the 1930s paintings of Regionalist artist Grant Wood. To apply what they learn, the students will examine their own identity in an essay and a collage.

The unit, *The Search for Identity,* exemplifies the use of an enduring idea for curriculum design and the integration of the arts. Although an English literature unit, its instructional purpose extends beyond teaching students about a significant American novelist or how to develop good essay writing skills. The Columbus High School English teacher who created the unit wrote:

"Those who settled in the West faced unique challenges in maintaining and establishing their identity. People today also face unique challenges toward the maintenance and establishment of an identity. This is a major concern of teenagers who are in the process of discovering and shaping their own identity. By reading Cather's novel, students begin to analyze the obstacles that the three main characters faced. This is the basis for writing assignments that focus on the topic of personal control over one's destiny."

The high school English students gain new perspectives about identity through exploring the expressions of a novelist and a painter, learn about subject matter which has strong personal connections for their own identity, acquire an understanding of the kinds of ideas and knowledge which can engage writers and artists in producing works of art, and, in general, increase their understanding that identity is a complex issue.

Source: Josette Kluck, Columbus High School, Columbus, Nebraska.

Johnson's claims are demonstrated in the following account of a discussion between a TETAC mentor and an elementary writing teacher about an integrated curriculum unit, "Bridges."[13] Although the unit was quite elaborate and incorporated knowledge and skills from social studies, language arts, science, and math, the TETAC mentor and the writing teacher discussed the possibilities of extending the bridges unit further in a metaphorical direction.

The Cleveland fourth graders who took part in this unit were studying local bridges, observing their structures and designs, capturing them in photographs, making drawings and three-dimensional models, writing essays and letters about bridges, investigating the history of Cleveland transportation and industry in relation to bridges, and preparing for a field trip to a local architect's office to conduct an interview about bridge design and engineering, and to participate in a riverboat tour of Cleveland's many bridges. In proposing a culminating project for the unit, the TETAC mentor suggested that the students might enlarge their understandings of bridges by thinking of them in metaphorical terms. Bridges are frequently cast in symbolic rather than literal terms, whether in ordinary conversation or art forms such as poetry, storytelling, dance, or visual expressions. The writing teacher immediately responded to this proposal, thinking of contemporary artist Faith Ringgold's story quilts and paintings *Tar Beach* and *Dancing on the George Washington Bridge*. In these works, the artist presents the bridge as a metaphor for personal dreams and aspirations. She imagined that the students might create their own dream bridges as metaphors for their personal aspirations and yearnings.

Although the students' study of bridges had been intensive, it was not until the arts were brought into the unit that the topic of bridges extended beyond the functional and practical. Metaphor is about finding new perspectives. Inserting the metaphorical into the bridge unit would have permitted learning to move into the area of human feelings. It is the arts that infuse the school curriculum with metaphorical understanding that might otherwise be overlooked. This is a compelling argument for including the arts as a key player in school curricula.

Art and the Aesthetic Dimensions of Knowing

The arts also bring another dimension to the learning experience: the aesthetic dimensions of knowing. Contemporary artists Ann Hamilton and James Turrell create interactive installations that capitalize on the sensory experiences as a portal to knowing the world. In 1991, Turrell created *Heavy Water*, a piece for a swimming pool in Poiters, France, that requires viewers to don a special suit and swim through an illuminated pool to a light-filled skyspace chamber at its center. Following this experience, participants have expressed feelings of resurrection and baptism.[15]

Writer Greer Pagano describes Hamilton's approach to aesthetic knowing:

Hamilton frequently, if not always, asks, through her work, what it means to be outside and what it means to be inside. The environments she creates reflect a constant investigation into the many forms and ways in which the body can be in and out of a space, as well as the multiple ways that relationships form between viewers and objects, images, movements, lights, and sounds.

Her works are always asking how it is that we use vision, text, smell, movement, and emotions to get closer to meaning . . . Hamilton forces the question— do I understand something because I can see it, read it, listen to it? What happens when those things become difficult? Does that affect my understanding? Again and again, these questions and the framework of the installations require recognition and planning of bodily movement, personal investigation of things that usually are obvious. Interaction with the space calls for an acknowledgement of embodied awareness.[16]

These examples exemplify and reinforce the significance of aesthetic knowing and how the arts can bring it into focus. In the following, we describe how the arts can amplify school learning through aesthetic dimensions of knowing.

Two Nebraska fourth-grade classroom teachers planned a science and art unit focused around the enduring idea of humans and nature and the topic of weather. The essential questions guiding the unit were (1) How do humans understand nature? (2) How does nature impact human behavior? and (3) How do humans affect nature?

In the unit, the students studied weather from a scientific perspective, learning about human attempts to understand and control nature through observation, measurement, and prediction. From an artistic perspective, the students observed and responded to paintings of the American West by painters Frederic Remington and Charles Russell, works that depict explorers and cowboys battling the natural elements of rain and snowstorms, intense desert temperatures, and river rapids. These images elicit emotional responses to nature that contrast with analytic scientific perspectives of natural phenomena. The visual clues and evidences of nature's assault on the figures in Remington and Russell's works developed understandings about the sensory and physical effects of nature on human life. Thus, in considering the same topic from different knowledge perspectives, students had an opportunity to learn that humans can and often do respond to the same phenomena in different ways.

In this chapter, we have endeavored to present arts learning as vital to the school curriculum and thus a consequential component in curriculum integration. In a study of the relationship of arts learning to the school curriculum and other school subjects conducted by Judith Burton and her colleagues Robert Horowitz and Hal Abeles, these researchers conclude:

What is critical is not that capacities and dispositions transfer from the arts to other subject areas, as has often been argued, but that they are exercised broadly across different knowledge domains. Given this interpretation, no subject has prior rights over any other subject, for to diminish one is to diminish the possibility and promise of them all. If the arts are to help define our path to the future, they need to become curriculum partners with other subject disciplines in ways that will allow them to contribute their own distinctive richness and complexity to the learning process as a whole.[17]

7.3 TETAC teachers from all subject areas, not only visual arts, spent much time investigating artists and artworks for curriculum integration.

FAQs

How can art curriculum be meaningfully integrated with social studies and the study of other cultures?

Frequently, art is integrated into the study of other cultures as an add-on or ancillary component rather than as an integral aspect that adds depth to learning. In several of the TETAC elementary schools, the study of other countries and cultures was a frequent theme. In these schools, the study of Asian, African, and South American cultures along with the study of other distant geographic locations became a part of the curriculum in every classroom. Often these elementary schools targeted a particular country to study for an entire year, with teachers collaboratively and individually designing units of study. It was a curriculum challenge to design these units of study as meaningful learning experiences. Finding a focus in the theme that would prevent learning from degenerating into a litany of facts about the targeted country was a major problem. The theme required contextualizing with a learning purpose that engaged students in substantive understanding about another culture
or society.

One solution, adopted by an Ohio TETAC school, was framing the study of a country with an enduring idea. They constructed the idea that all cultures have objects, artifacts, and performances that express their history, values, beliefs, and ways of life. The following essential questions guided this inquiry:

- What does this object, artwork, artifact, or performance tell about the past or present of this society?

- What does this object, artwork, artifact, or performance tell about the social ways of life (rituals, norms, behaviors), values, and beliefs of this society?

- What has caused change in the objects, artworks, artifacts, or performances of this society?

The use of this enduring idea and essential questions provided the teachers with a structure that organized a unit of study from myriad facts, events, and possible connections that could be part of learning about another culture. This strategy, selecting an enduring idea and essential questions to guide a schoolwide theme, could be utilized with any theme, not just one promoting study of other cultures.

These remarks mirror our intents in this chapter regarding art and curriculum integration. The arts need not become the centerpiece of the curriculum, but at the same time, they have a substantive role to play. We pointed to this role in describing metaphorical meaning and aesthetic knowing as distinctive characteristics of the arts. Metaphor and aesthetic knowing represent only two of the most unique qualities that the arts bring to the school curriculum; other contributions lie with imaginative, innovative, and flexible thinking skills and approaches to problem solving. However, if the arts are to foster such qualities, it is imperative that arts learning, as earlier recognized, be rigorous and substantive. A major factor in the effectiveness of curriculum integration resides in the quality of individual subject areas. A subject weakly represented in an individual instructional context will not be transformed under curriculum integration.

Notes

1   M. Parsons, "Art and Integrated Curriculum." In *Handbook of Research and Policy in Art Education,* eds. E. Eisner and M. Day (Mahwah, NJ: Lawrence Erlbaum, 2004), pp. 775–94.

2   The National Arts Education Consortium, *Transforming Education Through the Arts Challenge: Final Project Report* (Columbus, OH: Department of Art Education, The Ohio State University).

3   H. M. Kliebard, *The Struggle for the American Curriculum, 1893–1958.* 2nd ed. (London: Routledge, 1995); J. Dewey, *The School and Society; and The Child and the Curriculum* (Chicago: University of Chicago Press, 1990); original works published 1902.

4   K. Lake, "Close-up #16, Integrated Curriculum," School Improvement Research Series (SIRS), Northwest Regional Educational Laboratory (http://www.nwrel.org/scpd/sirs/8/c016.html). Other useful works on integrated curriculum include: J. A. Beane, *Curriculum Integration: Designing the Core of Democratic Education* (New York: Teachers College Press, 1997); R. Caine and G. Caine, *Making Connections: Teaching and the Human Brain* (Alexandria, VA: Association for Supervision and Curriculum, 1991); H. H. Jacobs, *Interdisciplinary Curriculum: Design and Implementation* (Alexandria, VA: Association for Supervision and Curriculum Development, 1989).

5   Parsons, "Art and Integrated Curriculum," pp. 775–94.

6   J. Burton, "The Arts in School Reform: Other Conversations," *Teachers College Record* 95, no. 4 (Summer 1994), p. 487. Burton's distinction is that "learning in art . . . involves engaging imaginatively with materials and processes, acquiring artistic concepts and skills that widen knowledge about self and culture and deepen critical-aesthetic sensibilities." On the other hand, she defines learning *through* art as an involvement "with themes and topics that lend themselves to contemplation and discovery from various vantage points, through various lenses which art is one among many."

7   Ibid.

8   H. H. Jacobs, *Interdisciplinary Curriculum: Design and Implementation* (Alexandria, VA: Association for Supervi-

sion and Curriculum Development, 1989)
(http://www.ascd.org/publications/books/1989jacobs/
jacobs_ch1.html).

9 O. Gude, "Investigating the Culture of Curriculum." In
   *Real-World Readings in Art Education: Things your Pro-
   fessor Never Told You,* eds. Dennis E. Fehr et al. (New
   York: Palmer Press, 2000) (http://www.uic.edu/classes/ad/
   ad382/sites/AEA/AEA_index.html).

10 A. D. Efland, *Art and Cognition* (New York: Teachers College Press, 2002), pp. 152–53.

11 Ibid., p. 153.

12 G. Lakoff and M. Johnson, *The Metaphors We Live By*
   (Chicago: University of Chicago Press, 1980), p. 193.

13 The unit "Bridges" was developed by Ms. Viriginia Wise-
   man at Newton D. Baker Elementary School of Arts,
   Cleveland, Ohio.

14 G. Lakoff, "The Contemporary Theory of Metaphor." In
   Metaphor and Thought, ed. Andrew Ortony (New York:
   Cambridge University Press, 1993), pp. 202–51.

15 L. M. Herbert, "Regarding Spirituality." In *Art:21: Art in
   the Twenty-first Century* (New York: Harry N. Abrams,
   Inc., 2001) pp. 68–118.

16 G. Pagano, "Anne Hamilton," unpublished essay, The
   Ohio State University, Department of Art Education,
   Columbus, OH, 2004, pp. 1–5.

17 J. Burton et al., "Learning in and through the Arts: Curriculum Implications." In *Champions of Change,* July
   1999, Center for Arts Education Research, Teachers College, Columbia University, unpaginated (http://artsedge.
   kennedy-center.org/champions/preface.html).

Chapter

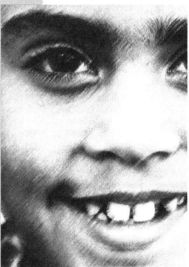

Visual Culture and the Curriculum

"Unless we click an off button or smash the screen, the images stream on . . ."
—Media theorist Todd Gitlin[1]

On a summer day not long ago, around forty art teachers roamed the aisles of the Target department store in Virginia Beach, Virginia. The art teachers were not shopping but rather observing displays, merchandise, customer and employee interactions, traffic patterns, sounds, signage, and aromas such as the strong smell of popcorn wafting through the air. The teachers were participants in a three-day institute, "The Next Wave: The World of Visual Culture," at the Contemporary Art Center of Virginia Beach, and this expedition to Target was motivated by the theme they were studying at the institute: the power of visual culture. The institute's theme was also featured in the art center's current exhibition, a display of surfboards, videotapes, photographs, and text panels recounting the history of surfing, prominent figures in the sport, and contemporary practices.[2]

Art Educator Talk

"We live in an increasingly image-saturated world where television news may control a person's knowledge of current events, where students spend more time in front of a screen than in front of a teacher, and where newborn babies are shown videos to activate still developing neurons."

Source: Kerry Freedman et al., "Curriculum Change for the 21st Century: Visual Culture in Art Education." In E. W. Eisner and M. D. Day (eds.), *Handbook of Research and Policy in Art Education* (Reston, VA: National Art Education Association, and Mahwah, NJ: Lawrence Erlbaum, Associates, 2004), pp. 815–28.

While the Contemporary Art Center exhibition and the art teacher institute both fall outside of conventional art concerns, they reflect trends in art education and the art world toward greater cultural relevance. Momentum for the inclusion of visual culture in art education has been mounting for some time as numerous scholars make their case for its relevance in the curriculum.[3] The content and activities of the summer art teacher institute reflected the widening conversation about what it means to live in an image-saturated culture. At the three-day institute, the art teachers and faculty explored the power of visual culture in everyday life through not only an investigation of the surfing exhibition and the trip to Target but also through a visit to the art center's parking lot to examine automobiles as signs of personal and social identity and a slide presentation of past and present artworks focused on the subject matter of society and the marketplace. As they considered what visual culture means for art curriculum and instruction, the art teachers and faculty explored four questions: (1) What is visual culture? (2) How does it shape our lives? (3) Why is it important to teach? and (4) How can we teach it in a meaningful way?

Visual culture was not a major curriculum focus for educators during the course of the TETAC project, but it has since become a leading concern throughout art education. In this chapter, we address some of the same questions art educators everywhere are now asking: (1) What is visual culture? (2) Why is it important for art learning? and (3) How can we teach it in a meaningful way?

What Is Visual Culture?

In some ways it is fairly obvious that visual culture refers to the images and objects we encounter on a daily basis such as signage, manufactured and hand-made objects, fashion, advertisements, film, computer

8.1 Artist, teacher, and designer Ed Obermeyer took part in "The Next Wave: The World of Visual Culture" at the Contemporary Art Center of Virginia Beach.

In the Classroom: Investigating the Commercial World

Art teachers explored a Target department store as part of a summer institute about visual culture held at The Contemporary Art Center of Virginia Beach. These activities could be adapted for students using other aspects of visual culture.

Target Activity I

Do this activity in groups of twos or threes.

Describe the visual culture you find at Target.

How is the visual culture at Target about . . . .

Display?	Aromas?	Temperature?	Sound?	Pathways?
Surfaces?	Style?	Social Class?	Gender?	Interaction?
Prohibitions?	Permissions?	Nonverbal language?	Verbal language?	Images?

Target Activity II

Do this activity individually.

Use your descriptions of visual culture at Target to interpret Target as an expression of contemporary visual culture. Look for contradictions and conflicts.

What does Target mean?

Target Activity III

Do this activity with a group.

Using the issue of power, find 5 objects that sell for $10 or less.

Object	How does the object represent power?
1.	
2.	
3.	
4.	
5.	

Buy one of the objects you listed above. Incorporate this object into a three-dimensional visual response/critique of Target as an expression of visual culture and power.

environments, television, and packaging. With such an extensive listing, we might ask instead, what is *not* visual culture? For many art education scholars, the term *culture* is as significant as the term *visual*. Including visual culture in the art curriculum does not simply mean covering a broader range of visual items that extend beyond traditional fine art categories; rather, it is about the cultural context that accompanies the visual as well. In Kerry Freedman's words, visual cul-

ture includes the "ideas, beliefs, and other conceptual realms that function in and around visual objects."[4] This is a significant point to be reckoned with in deliberating how visual culture has relevance for art education.

Art educators sometimes use the term *visuality* to explore the relationship between the cultural and the visual. John Walker and Sarah Chaplin explain that the meaning of this term goes beyond vision—the physical act of seeing. Visuality refers to a social process: vision

Lists: The Cultural Side of Seeing

The following is a list of concepts that help to explain how images work culturally. These concepts can inform art instruction about the images that infuse contemporary culture.

Learning to See Socially

- **Images are constructed**
  Although often they may appear natural and spontaneous, all images are constructed. Construction refers to the idea of pre-planning how an image will depict a particular subject. Advertisements are key examples of highly constructed images, but ones which often strive for a natural appearance. However, even personal photographs, snapshots, are constructed with social conventions.

- **Images are socially coded**
  Often images use social stereotypes and conventions to communicate. The visual has a social language that allows viewers to read images through stock visual conventions and often these stereotypical ideas are transferred to reality.

- **Images create reality**
  Images construct reality and this reality, as observed in the previous concept, can influence our notions of what reality is about. Television sitcoms are a good example of this concept. While often reduced to stereotypes and conventions, the everyday worlds portrayed in television sitcoms shape our notions of what families, friendships, romance, and occupations are about.

- **Images commodify the world**
  Both objects and persons are commodified through visual culture. For example, it is not a new revelation that professional sports are not simply about entertainment. Contemporary professional sports are as much about the product endorsements, the reflected team image for the sponsoring city, or the team logo branding everything from equipment to clothing to children's toys. Sports thus are a commodity. As with other celebrities, sports stars themselves have become commodities.

that has been socialized.[5] Art historian Norman Bryson also offers a description of visuality:

For human beings collectively to orchestrate their visual experience together it is required that each submit his or her retinal experience to the socially agreed description(s) of an intelligible world . . . Between the subject and the world is inserted the entire sum of discourses which make up visuality, the cultural construct; and makes visuality different from vision.[6]

We "see" images, objects, and events through preconceived ideas received from society. For example, when we see a McDonald's logo, we might be reminded of living in a culture of fast food and of the accompanying contradictions about health, obesity, and body image. We see the bright golden arches as part of our social culture, not simply as an attractive design element. Visuality holds for artworks as well. For instance, viewing an Andy Goldsworthy work, *Maple Patch* (1987)—a careful arrangement of maple leaves in hues ranging from bright yellow to dark ruby red—may appear to be a straightforward, "transparent" visual experience, but it is mediated by prior social experiences such as traditional art forms, abstraction, environmental concerns, and ideas about nature and culture. It is simply impossible to engage the visual without the social.

Photography as a Cultural Mediator

Essayist, critic, and novelist Susan Sontag recognized the decided impact that photography has had on our ways of seeing. In her 1977 book *On Photography*, Sontag recalled only really "seeing" a cathedral in Orvieto upon examining photographs of the cathedral.

When I was in Orvieto for the first time several months ago, I spent hours looking at the facade of the cathedral; but only when I bought a book on the cathedral a week later did I really see it, in the modern sense of seeing. The photographs enabled me to see in a way that my "naked" eye could not possibly see the "real" cathedral.[7]

As Sontag concluded, the camera changes our understandings of reality. As part of the art education curriculum, photography can provide an occasion for considering not only how contemporary photographic artworks suggest new versions of the world but also how cultural realities are presented in print publications, television, video, and on the Internet.

Art and Visual Culture

Should fine art be a category unto itself or does it belong as one among many categories under the umbrella of visual culture? And what difference would it make if we did or did not locate fine art as a subtopic under visual culture? Kerry Freedman and Patricia Stuhr acknowledge that "fine art is still of great value in education and an important part of historical and contemporary visual culture."[8] Art educator Peter Smith admonishes that "not to educate students about past and contemporary art that the teacher has learned to be valuable is to fall into that abdication of leadership that Dewey deplored and wished to see replaced by a sense of the duty and right to educate."[9]

In the Classroom

The following concepts from critic Susan Sontag suggest how the camera has altered contemporary views of reality. After applying these concepts to images from travel magazines, students recognized how strongly the tourist experience is entwined with photography, both personal and commercial.

- **Reality has come to seem more and more like what we are shown by cameras.**
  Students found that travel is motivated by images of escape, adventure, and exoticism.

- **Photography offers a crisis-proof experience.**
  Student discovered that capturing the experience with the camera mattered more than actually having an authentic experience.

- **The camera's rendering of reality must always hide more than it discloses.**
  Students realized that travel images were always idealized and non-problematic.

- **With photographs, we acquire something as information rather than as experience.**
  Again, students recognized that travel experiences were more about image than reality.

Source: S. Sontag, *On Photography* (New York: Doubleday, 1977).

What is the difference between everyday images/objects and artworks?

The following chart briefly presents some of the differences between everyday images/objects and artworks in terms of function and purpose.

Everyday Images/ Objects	Artworks
Functions	**Functions**
Entertain	Critique
Document	Aestheticize
Sell	Poeticize
Inform	Question
	Transcend
Consequences for Our Lives	**Consequences for Our Lives**
Create desire	Problematize
Create identity	Challenge
Stereotype	Transform
Commodity	Transcend
Objectify	
Produce social practices	
Establish norms	

Perhaps objective is the most significant difference between fine art and consumer and media culture. Discriminating among the different purposes of different types of visual culture is not a simple task. The same type of media, such as television, has many different purposes. For instance, the Weather Channel or cable news channels are not conceived with the same purpose as situation comedies or afternoon talk shows. Purpose matters. In general, consumer and material culture is created for purposes of commerce and entertainment. Artworks are generally created for more substantive expressive purposes, greater than filling a fashion season or an hour during prime time. Art critic Michael Rush remarks, "In other words, what is essential to the practice of art is the motivating idea possessed by the artist that questions existing codes or expressions, both in the world of art and in the culture at large."[10] For these reasons, we believe that although visual culture should be included in the art curriculum, artworks should continue to constitute its core.

And yet, we also recognize the pervasiveness of everyday images and objects, which most often register far greater impact on students' lives than do artworks. Kevin Tavin and other art educators contend that artworks alone are not sufficient to develop students' understandings of contemporary culture. Tavin notes how "numerous postmodern theories describe a new social order in which visual representations help mold and regulate social relationships, politics, race, gender, sexuality, and class"[11] Without the inclusion of visual representations beyond traditional fine art forms, art students would not be fully equipped to understand the contemporary world in terms of social relationships, politics, race, gender, sexuality, and class—all aspects of cultural understanding. Freedman similarly argues that images influence students' formation of identity and self-concepts.[12] She cites theorist Jacques Lacan, who claims that images function as the vehicle through which the ego or self is constructed and seeks completeness, albeit a completeness that never fulfils its promise.[13]

On the other side of the debate over including visual culture in the art curriculum are cultural theorists who have criticized contemporary imagery as being superficial, depthless, and self-referential. One of the most strident critics, Frederic Jameson, views images as complicit in the malaise that characterizes our consumer-driven society.[14] Jameson frequently employs the term *depthless* to characterize both non-art and art images. Guy Debord, an earlier theorist and critic of the 1960s, indicts consumer society's proliferation of images emptied of any reality and viewers who are passive recipients of mass-produced commodities.[15] This harsh criticism has been rejected by others who dispute the notion that "popular culture corrupts the masses through passive reception."[16]

Considering these perspectives, we would argue that not all media and images from consumer culture are inferior, just as not all fine art is good. A more valuable learning experience might be to encourage students to form their own judgments about the merits of the images they study. Consistent with the approach we advocate for allowing enduring ideas and key art understandings to shape art curricula, we do not believe it necessary or even possible to prescribe a finite list of images, objects, and events to be taught as subject content. Obviously, whether to draw on visual culture in choosing art content is a decision that will be made at the local level and will vary a great deal. Tavin notes that "while art educators place art from the museum realm at the center of their curriculum, their students are piecing together their expectations and dreams in and through popular culture."[17] He thus strongly supports the view that popular culture, as a major influence in the formation of values

Society of the Spectacle

Cultural theorist and activist Guy Debord's notion of contemporary culture as a society of the spectacle is an idea that continues to find resonance among other theorists in the arts and media attempting to explain the role of images in society today. Debord argues:

> ". . . the society of the spectacle" characterizes the modern period as an image-based culture entirely under the sway of the visual. In such circumstances, according to Debord, history is forgotten, the image is emptied of any reality, and viewers assume the role of passive consumers. The spectacle is not a collection of images, but rather social relations mediated by images.

Source: Guy Debord, *The Society of the Spectacle* (London: Black and Red, 1977).

In the Classroom: Car Talk

The following is an activity to reveal the connections between automobiles and personal identity. It is the subsequent discussion, based on the investigation of the automobiles, that has learning significance. It might be noted that the three perspectives—the personal, social, and historical—represent views that could provide a framework for looking at other examples of visual culture other than automobiles.

Finding Visual Culture in the Parking Lot

A small group activity.

Go to the parking lot and choose a car, but not one that belongs to someone in the group. Respond to the following questions:

Personal Perspective

Why might the owner/driver have chosen this car?

How could this car shape the identity of the driver?

Social Perspective

How does this car represent:
Class?
Gender?
Aesthetics?
Economics?
Political or social group?

Historical Perspective

How is the past represented in this car?

and beliefs, should be at the heart of students' experiences in art education.

In the following section, we provide an example of teaching the enduring idea of identity with two images, one from consumer culture and the other from fine art. Both address the same enduring idea of identity, and they complement one another in offering diverse perspectives on celebrity identity.

The Power of Images: Audrey Flack's *Marilyn* and a *Vogue* Cover

Cultural theorist W.J.T. Mitchell challenges the notion that visual culture means an end to the distinction between artistic and non-artistic images, that there will be a leveling of visual forms.[18] Mitchell suggests instead that visual culture can motivate reflection about the differences between art and non-art. It is this intersection that we believe holds much potential for art learning. As an example of what might be learned from encounters of this nature, one might compare a recent *Vogue* magazine cover, graced by the actress Renee Zellweger, with an Audrey Flack painting of the actress Marilyn Monroe, both of which address the enduring idea of identity—in these particular cases, celebrity identity.

Flack's portrait, *Marilyn* (1977), portrays the movie star not as the glamorous public figure she became but in the guise of her previous identity, as Norma Jean Mortenson. Composed in the style of a Dutch still life, Flack's work explores Monroe's identity through a traditional *vanitas* theme, evoking the transience of life and the ultimate corruption of beauty and the flesh. To depict this theme, Flack assembles among luxurious purple and mauve silks an assortment of ripe fruit, including a large grape cluster, pears, and a succulent orange and peach; photographs of the young Marilyn (Norma Jean Mortenson) surrounded by the tools of beauty—

a bright red lipstick, shiny compact with mirrored reflection of a small ornate perfume bottle, glossy red-orange rouge, and jade green eye shadow. Among these articles, Flack inserts signs connoting the passage of time—an hourglass, burning candle, pocket watch, and calendar. This combination of elements allows viewers to speculate on the meanings of the life of an actress who died mysteriously at age thirty-six and about the larger connotations of human existence itself.

The *Vogue* cover portrays Zellweger as a glamorous and sensuous figure, a generic representation that could have been filled by any number of popular actresses. Zellweger lounges in a garden environment attired in a very feminine dress, on the order of a Monet painting, posed with a highly seductive facial expression, head lowered and eyes suggestively entreating viewers. The image teaches almost nothing about Zellweger herself or about life. The two representations, Monroe and Zellweger, are animated by different purposes, one to delve into the ultimate meanings about life and the other to promote and sell a popular publication.

In the classroom, a comparison of this sort could become an opportunity for considering the power of images. The Flack portrait peels away the veneer of the stereotypical celebrity identity to motivate viewers to contemplate what celebrity and life are really all about. The Zellweger image has power of a different sort. Replicating and reinforcing stereotypical notions of glamour and fame, the image might be said to produce unrealistic desires for the unattainable. Each of these images, the Flack painting and the *Vogue* cover, situates the viewer differently. The *Vogue* cover distances viewers because we cannot attain that which is represented, leaving us with unrealizable desires; whereas the Flack portrait engages

Lists: Images/Objects of Visual Culture

toys	painting
posters	fast-food paraphernalia
advertisements	hairdryers
CD covers	furniture
sculpture	street signage
movies	installations
video games	fashion
cable television programs	textiles
Internet sites	automobiles
children's books	garden design
breakfast cereal boxes	typography
architecture	ceramics

8.2 Audrey Flack, Marilyn (Vanitas), *1977. Oil and acrylic on canvas, 96" x 96" (244 x 244 cm). Courtesy Louis K. Meisel Gallery, New York. Photo by Steven Lopez.*

Museum or Showroom?
The Art World and the Commercial World

In the summer of 1998, the Solomon R. Guggenheim Museum inaugurated the Guggenheim Las Vegas with its exhibition The Art of the Motorcycle. Displaying over 130 motorcycles, the show, sponsored by BMW, chronicled the evolution of the motorcycle from its beginnings with Michaux-Perreaux (1868) to the most advanced models of the present day. The exhibition drew record-breaking crowds in Las Vegas and also when the exhibition traveled to the Field Museum of Natural History in Chicago and the Guggenheim Bilbao, Spain.

The online site for the Guggenheim exhibition defends the presentation, remarking that, "the motorcycle is an immortal cultural icon that changes with the times. More than speed, it embodies the abstract themes of rebellion, progress, freedom, sex, and danger. The limits imposed by its possible forms and functions, and the breadth of variation that has been expressed within these limitations, provide a framework in which to examine the motorcycle both as object and as emblem of our century." Others were not as enthusiastic. The Web site Motorcycle Online comments, "Some critics have dismissed the Art of the Motorcycle as shameless capitulation to popular and corporate culture, and within motorcycle circles there is debate whether or not motorcycles rise to the level of art or are simply the product of creative and inspired industrial design."

Sources: The Art of the Motorcycle, "Introduction" (http://www.guggenheim.org/exhibitions/past_exhibitions/motorcycle/motorcycle.html). Motorcycle.com, "The Art of the Motorcycle" (www.motorcycle.com/mo/mcmuseum/gug.html).

8.3 The motorcycle is a cultural icon that has found its way from the showroom to the museum. Photo by Marilyn Stewart.

the viewer with notions that pertain to all of humanity, not just to a select few.

Engaging Art, Self, and the World
Since the mid-1990s, W.J.T. Mitchell has taught a course called Visual Culture at the University of Chicago. Of this experience he declares that "the point of a course in visual culture . . . would be to provide students with a set of critical tools for the investigation of human visuality, not to transmit a specific body of information and values."[19] Mitchell's assertion resonates with our goals for art curriculum and learning. Because the curriculum can never cover all the specific content that students should know and understand about art, the purpose of a curriculum should be to focus on the processes of learning, giving students, to use Mitchell's terminology, a set of critical tools for investigating art, the self, and the world.

Recall Chapter 4, "Making Choices: Selecting Lesson Content to Build on Unit Foundations," in which we focused on art learning through the principles and concepts of art criticism, art history, artmaking, and aesthetics. Similarly, we approach learning about visual culture by offering strategies that students can use to engage visual culture in a meaningful manner. The art criticism and artmaking principles and concepts articulated in Chapter 4 (see the sidebars on pages 44 and 53, respectively) could be employed as critical tools for investigating visual culture. Tavin suggests having students inquire, What investments do we have in certain images? What do we learn from these images? What do the images not teach? Do these images help mobilize desire, anger, or pleasure in us? Do we believe these images embody sexist, racist, ablest [sic], and class-specific interests?"[20]

According to Mitchell, the experience of seeing is veiled with a familiarity and self-evidence that prevents students from understanding how the visual works. He explains it as a paradox that vision is itself invisible. Mitchell takes it as his task to "make seeing show itself, to put it on display, and make it accessible for analysis."[21] In the next section we suggest four strategies to be employed as critical tools for unveiling seeing. To explain how to use these tools, we end by presenting an instructional unit based on the enduring idea of identity and belonging. Artist Nikki S. Lee's *Projects* and a teenage skateboard publication, *Thrasher,* serve as the content focus of this unit.

The Enduring Idea and Visual Culture

The enduring idea of identity and belonging represents a concept of import for adolescent students in middle school and high school. Nikki S. Lee, a contemporary artist who delves into issues associated with being a member of specific groups, is a strong subject choice for this investigation because her work is

Four Critical Tools for Investigating Visual Culture

1 Language
Considering how language both shapes and reflects understanding is an important critical tool for investigating visual culture.

- Everyday
- Metaphorical
- Slang
- Marketplace
- Technical
- Personal

2 The Personal
Considering how the personal shapes and reflects understanding is an important critical tool for investigating visual culture.

- Memory contributes to a personal construction of understanding.
- Experience contributes to personal constructions of understanding.
- Beliefs and values contribute to personal constructions of understanding.

3 The Social
Considering how social context shapes understanding is an important critical tool for investigating visual culture, particularly for expanding understanding beyond the personal.

- The social can include social practices, norms, conventions, beliefs, values, and ideas as well as institutions and organizations.

4 Inquiry
Considering significant questions is an important critical tool for developing understanding about visual culture.

- A few key questions can open up unrealized perspectives.

directly concerned with the enduring idea and reflects contemporary culture. The skateboard magazine *Thrasher,* popular among adolescents interested in the sport, offers a different view about what it means to be a part of a social group and directly links the enduring idea with an element of social reality.

Skateboard Culture

Skateboarding is a social activity that takes place on neighborhood streets, in skate parks, and in touring performances and competitions. In 2004, CNN estimated that there were 12 million skateboarders nationwide and more than a thousand public skate parks, in addition to the multitude of private ones. *Thrasher* magazine represents one aspect of this phenomenon, and features a mix of highly skilled professional and semiprofessional skateboarders.

Nikki S. Lee

In her photographic *Projects,* Lee documents herself as a member of a variety of groups such as tourists, seniors, yuppies, Hispanics, exotic dancers, and skateboarders among others. As a young Korean-American artist, Lee is not a natural member of these groups.

8.4 *The images and objects of skateboard culture offer a unique view about what it means to be a part of a social group. Top right: Nikki S. Lee,* The Skateboarders Project (29), *2000. Fujiflex print. Bottom right: Nikki S. Lee,* The Skateboarders Project (1), *2000. Fujiflex print.*

Skateboarder's Talk

Tricks for Skateboarding

Air: riding with all four wheels off the ground; short for "aerial"

Backside: when a trick or turn is executed with the skater's back facing the ramp or obstacle.

Carve: to skate in a long, curving arc

Fakie: skating backward—the skater is standing in his or her normal stance, but the board is moving backward (not to be confused with "switch stance")

Frontside: when a trick or turn is executed with the front of the skater's body facing the ramp or obstacle

Goofyfoot: riding with the right foot forward, the opposite of "regular foot"

Grind: scraping one or both axles on a curb, railing, or other surface, such as:

  Crooked grind: grinding on only the front truck while sliding

  50-50 grind: grinding on both trucks equally

Nosegrind: grinding on only the front truck

5-0 grind: grinding on only the back truck

Mongo-foot: a style of pushing where the back foot is kept on the board and pushing is done with the front foot

Ollie: a jump performed by tapping the tail of the board on the ground; the basis of most skating tricks

Railslide: a trick in which the skater slides the underside of the deck along an object, such as a curb or handrail

Regular foot: riding with the left foot forward, the opposite of "goofyfoot"

Switch stance: riding the board with the opposite footing than usual, i.e., "goofyfoot" instead of "regular foot"

Tailslide: sliding the underside of the tail end of a board on a ledge or lip

Source: www.exploratorium.edu/skateboarding/largeglossary.html

She had to develop a relationship with those who already were participants in, as one writer describes, "closed communities." She acquired the physical appearance and body language of punk rockers, tourists, young Hispanic women, exotic dancers, and elderly seniors and participated in group activities such as skateboarding on neighborhood streets, dancing in strip clubs, and hanging wet clothes on clotheslines in the backyard of a New York Hispanic neighborhood. Lee took up residence with these groups for weeks or even months at a time. Although she explained to group members that she was there as an artist documenting her inclusion into their group, Lee relates that frequently group members more or less forgot or didn't really understand what she was about.

Critical Strategies: Language

Having determined an enduring idea and selected two aspects of visual culture for investigating this enduring idea, what would be the next steps in terms of planning instruction?

8.5 *Dee Van Dyke,* Signs of Life, *c. 6' x 10" (183 x 26 cm): Artist Dee Van Dyke combines everyday traffic signs with her own figurative forms. These signs were exhibited at the BMW showroom in Dusseldorf, Germany in 1992.*

The four critical tools listed in the sidebar on page 133 can be used to engage students in investigating visual culture. We begin with language. Students might brainstorm terms that describe the idea of belonging, such as *conformity, status, security, appearance, codes, rules, inclusion, exclusion, popularity, desire, choice,* and *commitment.* Students could discuss these terms in relation to the idea of identity. The instructional goal would be to for students to discover how social belonging is a significant aspect of identity. As art critic Barry Schwabsky deduces about Lee's *Projects,* "there may be eight million stories in the Naked City, but the number of social identities we recognize and inhabit is far fewer. Some are self-selected (punk rockers, for instance), some apparently ascriptive (Hispanics), some even combinations of both (say, young Japanese in the East Village). What matters is being part of a group, not condemned to go it alone."[22]

Critical Strategies: Personal Connections

Once students begin to understand that the sense of belonging is a substantial factor in shaping identity, they might then consider this idea in connection to their own lives. Students could use the following questions to examine a social group, formal or informal, to which they belong:

- Why would someone be excluded or included in this group?
- What are the expectations for appearance?
- What are the expectations for behavior?
- What values are important to group members?
- What are the visible signs of this group?
- What are the evidences of conformity in this group?
- What are the evidences of individuality in this group?

In the Classroom: Tourism

Language

In an instructional unit about tourism, students brainstormed words associated with tourism and linked them to the terms *identity, desire, norms, stereotypes, commodify,* or *experience.* They found that the majority of the words were associated with experience suggesting that travel is about 'having an experience.'

Travel Publications

Students placed one of the terms, *identity, desire, norms, stereotypes, commodify,* or *experience* with various images taken from travel magazines and discussed why they associated these terms with each of the images.

Artworks

Students examined Duane Hanson's photo-realistic sculpture, *Tourists* (1970) comparing it with Nikki S. Lee's photographs from her *Tourist Project* (1997), recognizing many stereotypes of tourism in both artists' works. Students learned of Native American performance artist James Luna's performance piece *Take a Picture with a Real Indian* (1991), which questions the authenticity of the tourist experience by having members of the audience decide which of three different cut-out versions of Luna is real: the "real Indian," constructed of stereotypes; the artist in street clothes; or the artist wearing the Plains Indian attire that tourists expect all Indians to wear all the time. The tourist experience acquires personal validity through the camera. Luna objects to the stock, stereotypic tourist photograph, a representation of falsity, while tourists conversely view it as evidence of their experience.

Artmaking

Armed with throwaway cameras, students visited known tourist sites in their town of Virginia Beach and shot photographs role-playing tourists. Returning to the art room with their developed photographs, the students created a set of six postcards that were designed to alter the viewer's perception of tourism in Virginia Beach.

Social Context: Interpreting Skateboard Culture

Now that students have engaged the enduring idea of identity and belonging, they can use their new understandings to investigate *Thrasher.* How will students investigate this form of visual culture and for what purpose? The previous activities, brainstorming language about identity and belonging and exploring personal connections, should have provided students with a useful knowledge base for investigating the images and text of the skateboard magazine. Importantly, students should center on the particular messages that the magazine conveys about skateboarders, not what they already believe to be true about skateboarders. As a later point of discussion, students can pursue the differences they find in the publication's representation of skateboarders and their own experiences and knowledge, as well as speculate why the publication is invested in this particular representation; but first students must establish the publication's views.

Students might work in small groups, supplied with a dozen or so pages from *Thrasher,* and apply the same questions from the previous exercise about their personal membership in social groups. Using these broad questions about social groups and belonging that apply to multiple contexts provides students with a process for learning. In the case of identity and belonging, the questions explore group expectations regarding image, behavior, attitudes, and values.

The question of what group values are exhibited in this publication can be explored numerous times in this publication. For example, emblazoned across a montage of skater snapshots was the text ". . . was fun except for all the babies that were in it . . . skaters don't cry." This is just one instance of many images and text in which the publication resoundingly portrays skateboarding as a highly macho culture, often reinforced with coarse language and numerous depictions of daredevil stunts.

As students look for evidence of conformity and individuality in this group, they may be surprised to find how many of the skateboard images are premised upon stock poses of skaters precariously careening down handrails or flying down concrete slopes. Hairstyles, clothing, body language, and attitudes all exhibit strong evidence of conformity among members of this group.

The publication also contains a massive amount of advertising, often a mirror image of the text and images accompanying the articles, so much so that it can be difficult to distinguish between the two. Students can investigate the commercial side of group identification, noting the importance of outward signs such as having the right clothing, shoes, and equipment. Additionally, such advertisements connote the proper body language and attitude one should assume as a member of this group as well.

How do these images and text position the viewer? Often we fail to realize that images position us in particular ways, that they create a particular relationship between us and the subject. Since *Thrasher* conveys strong connotations of what it means to be a member of an elite macho group of skilled skaters, it should not be difficult for students to recognize how they are positioned by the publication. For instance, female students will realize that in this culture they are mostly invisible or else positioned as spectators or sexual objects, but certainly not as participants. Nonskaters, and even skaters, may perceive themselves as outsiders, since the skill levels portrayed in the magazine exceed those of everyday skaters. The macho language and behavior may lead students to question not only the skateboard culture but their own values and beliefs as well.

Seeing is about both viewing and being viewed. Jacques Lacan refers to the reciprocal nature of seeing as the gaze *("le regard")*. For Lacan, seeing is subjective and cannot be separated from the self. Awareness of how images position us as viewers is part of understanding this relationship as a two-way dialogue. Middle school and high school students learn this by considering how an image reveals their own relationship to the subject depicted.

Artworks: Nikki S. Lee's Projects

The inclusion of Nikki S. Lee's work introduces further perspectives about belonging and identity. Lee's assimilation into diverse groups attends more to the general idea of group identity than the specifics of a particular group. For instance, if someone like Lee can so easily slip into and out of different groups, what is belonging about? Art critic Barry Schwabsky contends,

For Lee, it seems, these identities are all fundamentally subject to convention; absentminded viewers might be fooled, but she is not deceiving the people whose lives she is temporarily sharing: After all, there's no way this Korean could convince a group of Latinos, for example, that she's one of them, though it is quite possible for them to act as if that were the case. The people who pose with Lee are her collaborators, but they don't have to understand why she's doing what she does; they only need to be willing to play along.

If, as Schwabsky asserts, group members are only playing along, what does this tell us about groups

In the Classroom: Garden Culture

March 23, 2004

From: Goodlettsville Elementary Garden Design Committee

To: All Interested Artists/Gardeners

Subject: Garden Design Commission

Dear Artist/Gardener:

The Garden Design Committee invites you to submit a garden design proposal. We understand that you have studied the work of Isamu Noguchi and the Getty Garden by Robert Irwin. We would like for you to consider these artists when designing your garden for Goodlettsville Elementary. You can incorporate design elements from one or both of these artists. Please include a written explanation of which artists have influenced your design and why. Attached you will find images of the space for which you are designing.

Thank you for your time and we look forward to seeing your proposal.

GES Garden Design Committee—2004

Why would an art teacher spend a considerable amount of instructional time with this garden project?

Mindy Conley, who teaches art at Goodlettsville Elementary, offers this rationale:

> *"The topic of gardens presents an engaging and age-appropriate bridge into the big idea of humans and nature. Generally, the students at Goodlettsville Elementary come from rural and suburban settings. Their experiences with nature and gardens are possibly limited. A student's concept of art, gardens, and the creative process can be broadened by learning about artists who 'sculpt' the garden space and by considering their own design for a site-specific garden at school. As an educator, I feel it is very important to give students experiences that help them realize they have options for improving their lives and circumstances."*

During the unit, the following questions were central to the many unit activities that engaged the third graders:

What makes a garden a garden?

Should there be parameters?

When/where does a garden end and nature, in general, begin?

What can be included in a garden?

What can't be included in a garden?

Activities that preceded the third grader's garden planning included:

- Brainstorming what the students already knew about gardens.
- Linking images of various types of gardens, (flower gardens, vegetable gardens, formal gardens, Japanese dry gardens, topiary gardens, and rooftop gardens) with descriptive language.
- Creating garden journals.
- Studying Robert Irwin's *Getty Garden* and Isamu Noguchi's Japanese dry gardens.
- Creating small dry gardens in aluminum pie plates.
- Viewing a PowerPoint presentation of sesasonal gardens, inspirational gardens and local gardens in their community of Nashville, Tennessee.
- Inspecting the school site for their garden proposals.
- Creating plans and a rationale for the school garden.

and belonging? Lee herself views transitioning from group to group as a way of finding new identities and the possibilities of new selves. She believes that individual identity is fluid and a matter of context. Although Lee views her belonging to a group as positive, others may see her movement from group to group as masquerade and one of superficial adaptation. Her perspective challenges those who view identity as composed of an essential self that might have to be relinquished in part or whole in exchange for group inclusion.

Lee's unexpected actions, temporarily joining unfamiliar communities, serves as a catalyst for rethinking what students may take for granted. It is not the visual which is unveiled in this instance, as Mitchell admonished, but the social context itself. Belonging to social groups is a major aspect of teen-age culture and examining Lee's works may stimulate student reflection on what this is about in their own lives. If such questions are not raised, then her work becomes little more than gimmickry.

Reflection

Why did the unit need to include both the publication from popular culture and the work of an artist? Would the students' learning experience have been diminished by the exclusion of either of these visual events? The skateboard magazine demonstrated the shaping of group identity through the visual in everyday life. It presented belonging and identity with this group as something desirable. Lee's *Projects* unearthed broad questions about group identity. Together, these works prompted students to confront their understandings of self and the world.

Our intent in this chapter has been to acknowledge visual culture as a significant issue in art education curriculum and lay out some of the possibilities for its

inclusion. Other fields such as media studies and cultural studies have also produced writings with significance for art teachers who want to develop their knowledge and understanding about the area of visual culture.[23]

Notes

1   T. Gitlin, *Media Unlimited: How the Torrent of Images and Sounds Overwhelms Our Lives* (New York: Henry Holt and Co., 2002), pp. 20–21.

2   The 2003 Virginia Beach Contemporary Art Center teacher institute was planned and implemented by art education professors Stephen Carpenter of Virginia Commonwealth University, Marilyn Stewart of Kutztown University, and Sydney Walker of Ohio State University; Art Coordinator for Virginia Beach Public Schools, Anne Wolcott; and museum educator for the Contemporary Art Center of Virginia Beach, Ragan Cole-Cunningham.

3   T. Barrett, "Interpreting Visual Culture," *Art Education 56,* no. 2, 2003, pp. 6–13; P. Duncum, "A Case for an Art Education of Everyday Aesthetic Experiences," *Studies in Art Education* 40, no. 4, 1999, pp. 295–311; P. Duncum and T. Bracey, eds., *On Knowing: Art and Visual Culture* (Christchurch, New Zealand: Canterbury University Press, 2001); P. Duncum, "Visual Culture in the Classroom," *Art Education* 56, no. 2, 2003, pp. 25–32; K. Freedman and P. Stuhr, "Curriculum Change for the 21st Century: Visual Culture in Art Education," *Handbook of Research and Policy in Art Education,* eds. E. W. Eisner and M. D. Day (Mahwah, NJ: Lawrence Erlbaum, 2004), pp. 815–28; K. Freedman, *Teaching Visual Culture* (New York: Teachers College Press, 2003); D. Krug, "Symbolic Culture and Art Education," *Art Education* 56, no. 2, 2003, pp. 13–19; J. Marshall, "Articulate Images: Bringing the Pictures of Science and Natural History into the Art Curriculum," *Studies in Art Education* 45, no. 2, 2004, pp. 135–52; P. Smith, "Visual Culture Studies versus Art Education," *Arts Education Policy Review* 104, no. 4 (March/April 2003), pp. 3–8; K. Tavin, "The Impact of Visual Culture on Art Education: Teaching in and through Visual Culture," *The Journal of Multi-*

cultural and Cross-cultural Research in Art Education 18, no. 1, 2000, pp. 20–23, 37–40; K. Tavin, "Engaging Advertisements: Looking for Meaning in and through Art Education," *Visual Arts Research* 28, no. 2, 2002, pp. 38–47; S. R. Walker, "Artmaking in an Age of Visual Culture: Vision and Visuality," *Visual Arts Research,* December 2004.

4   K. Freedman, *The Journal of Multicultural and Cross-cultural Research in Art Education* 18, no. 1, 2000, pp. 41–44.

5   J. Walker and S. Chaplin, *Visual Culture: An Introduction* (New York: Manchester University Press, 1997), p. 22.

6   N. Bryson, "The Gaze in the Expanded Field." In *Vision and Visuality,* ed. H. Foster (Seattle, WA: Bay View Press/ Dia Art Foundation, 1988), pp. 91–94.

7   G. Movius, "An Interview with Susan Sontag," Boston Review, 1975 (http://www.bostonreview.net/BR01.1/ sontag.html).

8   K. Freedman and P. Stuhr, "Curriculum Change for the 21st Century."

9   P. Smith, "Visual Culture Studies versus Art Education," p. 6.

10 M. Rush, "The Conceptual Body," *Video Art* (London: Thames & Hudson, 2003), p. 72.

11 K. Tavin, "The Impact of Visual Culture on Art Education," pp. 37–40.

12 K. Freedman, "The Importance of Student Artistic Production to Teaching Visual Culture," *Art Education* 56, no. 2, March 2003, pp. 38–43.

13 J. Lacan, *The Four Fundamental Concepts of Psychoanalysis,* ed. Jacques-Alain Miller and trans. Alan Sheridan (New York: W. W. Norton & Co., 1981).

14 F. Jameson, *Postmodernism or the Cultural Logic of Late Capitalism* (Durham: Duke University Press, 1991), chapter 1.

15 G. Debord, *Society of the Spectacle,* trans. Donald Nicholas-Smith, 1994 (New York: Zone Books, 1995/1967).

16 K. Tavin, "Wrestling with Angels, Searching for Ghosts: Toward a Critical Pedagogy of visual culture," *Studies in Art Education* 4, no. 3), 2003, p. 199.

17 Ibid., pp. 197–213.

18 W.J.T. Mitchell, "Showing Seeing: A Critique of Visual Culture," *Art History, Aesthetics, Visual Studies,* ed. Michael Ann Holly and Keith Moxey (New Haven: Yale University Press, 2002), pp. 231–50.

19 W.J.T. Mitchell, "What Is Visual Culture?" In *Meaning in the Visual,* ed. I. Lavin (Princeton, NJ: Institute for Advanced Study, 1995), p. 207.

20 K. Tavin, "Wrestling with Angels, Searching for Ghosts," p. 208.

21 W.J.T. Mitchell, "Showing Seeing," pp. 231–32.

22 B. Schwabsky, (September, 1999). Nikki S. Lee, *Artforum (*URL: http://www.findarticles.com/ p/articles/mi_m0268/is_1_38/ai_55939337).

23 M. Andrejevic, *Reality TV: The Work of Being Watched* (New York: Rowman & Littlefield Publishers, Inc., 2004); J. T. Caldwell, *Televisuality: Style, Crisis, and Authority in American Television* (New Brunswick, NJ: Rutgers University Press, 1995); J. Fisherkeller, *Growing Up with Television: Everyday Learning among Young Adolescents* (Philadelphia, PA: Temple University Press, 2002); D. Gauntlett, *Video Critical: Children, the Environment, and Media Power* (Bedfordshire, England: University of Luton Press/John Libby Media, 1996); T. Gitlin, *Media Unlimited,* pp. 20–21; b. hooks, *Reel to Real: Race, sex, and Class at the movies* (New York: Routledge, 1996); N. Mirzoeff, *An Introduction to Visual Culture* (New York: Routledge, 1999); W.J.T. Mitchell, "Showing Seeing," pp. 231–49; M. J. Smith and A. F. Wood, *Survivor Lessons: Essays on Communication and Reality Television* (Jefferson, NC: McFarland & Company, Inc., 2003), S. Sontag, *On Photography* (New York: Farrar, Straus and Giroux, 1977); J. A. Walker, *Art in the Age of Mass Media,* rev. ed. (London: Pluto Press, 1994).

Appendix

Appendix A: Guidelines for Developing Comprehensive Art Education Units

These guidelines, adapted from those used by teachers involved with the TETAC project, can be used in the planning and evaluation of units of instruction according to the ideas presented in this book.

Unit Foundations

- *Does the unit address enduring ideas about the human experience?*
  Enduring ideas are those that have appeared to be of continual concern to humans at different times in different cultures. These are the ideas that are taught and retaught throughout the unit.

- *Does the unit address enduring ideas about art?*
  Enduring ideas about art are those that are key to connecting and understanding knowledge through the arts. These are ideas that are taught and retaught throughout the unit.

- *Does the unit address key concepts and essential questions?*
  Key concepts and essential questions are derived from interpreting artworks in the context of the enduring ideas of the unit.

- *Are the unit objectives, instructional activities, and assessment tasks aligned?*
  Initial planning is required to align what students will learn, how they will learn it, and how learning will be assessed.

- *Are the unit objectives aligned with national, state, and/or local standards?*
  Requirements for alignment with standards may vary among districts.

Unit Content

- *Are the disciplines of art/areas of inquiry developed in the unit to foster understanding of the enduring idea and key concepts?*
  In order to construct deep understanding of the enduring idea and key concepts, it is important to engage students in artmaking, art criticism, art-historical inquiry, and philosophical inquiry (aesthetics).

- *Does the unit sufficiently address the knowledge and skills that students need to develop deep understanding of the enduring idea and key concepts?*
  It is important to plan for sufficient instruction so that students have the knowledge base and requisite skills to construct deep understanding.

- *Does the unit address the knowledge and skills in a logical sequence to achieve unit objectives?*
  Students need to be guided through learning activities in a logical manner, building upon prior knowledge and skills, in order to meet unit objectives.

- *Are key concepts and important terms introduced and sufficiently developed?*
  Students need to explore examples and non-examples of important terms and make connections to their own experiences in order to understand concepts.

- *Do the enduring ideas, key concepts, and essential questions provide focus and cohesiveness throughout the unit?*

The enduring ideas, key concepts, and essential questions are revisited throughout the unit. All topics need to support and not detract from understanding.

- *Are content and skills appropriate for student developmental levels?*
  Content should reflect student ability and interest levels.

- *Are specific, substantive connections between art and other subject areas developed as appropriate?*
  Connections should be meaningful and enrich both art and other subject areas.

Instruction

- *Do activities and questions provide substantive engagement for students?*
  Activities and questions yield multiple answers and solutions, leading students to develop their own questions and understandings. Activities and questions can be explored again and again.

- *Are connections to prior knowledge and skills and real-life situations provided?*
  Meaningful connections to real-life situations will engage students more fully.

- *Are students made aware of assessment expectations?*
  Students should be informed of assessment criteria/expectations in the initial stages of instruction.

- *Are opportunities provided for students to practice new skills and use new concepts?*
  Ample time should be provided for students to practice skills and apply new concepts.

- *Are opportunities provided for students to ask questions?*
  Inquiry should be welcomed. Students need to be taught how to ask questions so that they might generate questions to guide their own investigations.

- *Are opportunities provided for student-led discussions?*
  Students need to be provided with strategies for engaging in discussions and with opportunities to practice. They need to be given tools/guides for focusing and/or evaluating their discussions.

- *Are students provided a variety of opportunities to make individual and collaborative contributions to the group effort?*
  In the course of a unit, students work independently and in groups, using a variety of strategies, resources, and materials.

- *Are students provided opportunities for self-reflection and meta-cognition?*
  Students should have models of and opportunities for thinking, talking, and writing about their own thinking.

- *Are students provided with opportunities for critical thinking?*
  Students need to be given instruction in critical thinking strategies; e.g., analysis, problem solving, interpretation, and evaluation.

- *Is there an audience for student work and responses?*
  Peers, parents, and community audiences add relevance to student work, increase engagement, and help students make connections beyond the classroom.

- *Are materials and resources appropriate for student developmental levels?*
  Reading levels, concept levels, tools, materials, and resources should be appropriate.

Assessment

- *Are enduring ideas, key concepts, and important skills assessed?*
  Significant/targeted knowledge and skills should be assessed.

- *Are assessment tasks accompanied by specific criteria?*
  Students may examine their work over time in a unit, use different kinds of criteria, and/or be given the opportunity to develop the criteria with the teacher. Rating scales and rubrics should be provided for students when appropriate.

- *Are assessment tasks relevant and engaging to students?*
  Assessment tasks frequently allow for multiple answers and solutions. Assessment allows for the application of a repertoire of skills and knowledge.

- *Are students provided opportunities to provide evidence of learning?*
  Assessment can occur through formative and summative strategies and tasks.

- *Are students provided opportunities for self-assessment?*
  When students are made aware of expectations, they can be included in the process of determining the extent to which they have achieved them.

Unit Design

- *Are the key unit and lesson components included and presented clearly?*
  Formats vary, but unit and lesson components should be included so that any teacher can easily understand the unit foundations, content, instruction, and assessment.

- *Are units centered on ideas about art and/or specific artworks or artifacts?*
  Artworks chosen as exemplars throughout the unit should represent or express the enduring ideas, key concepts, and essential questions of the unit.

- *Are objectives stated so as to indicate learning (knowledge, skills) and not simply as descriptions of activities in which students will be engaged?*
  Objectives should indicate the understandings, knowledge, and skills that students will demonstrate.

- *Does the unit provide opportunities for students to explore a relevant and diverse range of art and artists?*
  Selection of artworks and artists studied in the unit should be relevant (to the students and to the enduring ideas and key concepts) and diverse (in terms of culture, time, gender, age, language, and/or points of view).

- *Are emerging/developing technologies utilized in a variety of ways that promote effective learning?*
  Technology components should be meaningful, not trivial.

- *Are the necessary resources and materials for teaching the unit listed?*
  The availability of resources such as reproductions, Web sites, and others should be considered when planning units.

- *Are community resources, such as museums, galleries, theaters, resident artists, etc., identified and utilized when possible?*
  Community resources (human and material) can be used in meaningful ways.

Appendix B: Six Approaches to Unpacking Enduring Ideas

Here are six ways for unpacking enduring ideas in the classroom to develop students' understanding of them.

1 Questions
Significant questions are a major tool for unpacking enduring ideas.

A few essential questions about the enduring idea can help to keep a unit on track and focused.

2 Language
Language shapes and reflects our understandings of enduring ideas.

We can develop categories for language that shapes and reflects an enduring idea:
- everyday
- slang
- technical
- metaphorical
- marketplace
- personal

3 The Personal
The personal shapes and reflects our understanding of enduring ideas.

- Memory contributes to personal constructions of enduring ideas.
- Experience contributes to personal constructions of enduring ideas.
- Beliefs and values contribute to personal constructions of enduring ideas.

4 The Social
The social context shapes and reflects our understandings of enduring ideas.

- The social is important for expanding enduring ideas beyond the personal.
- The social can include social practices, norms, conventions, beliefs, values, and ideas as well as institutions and organizations.

5 Art
Art shapes and reflects our understandings of enduring ideas.

- Artists and artworks from diverse cultures and time periods can inform understanding of enduring ideas.
- Contemporary artworks often possess particular relevance for informing understandings about big ideas.

6 Visual Culture
Visual culture shapes and reflects our understandings of enduring ideas.

Visual culture can include:
- Mass media: television, movies, magazines, signage
- The physical environment: architecture, retail display, apparel, interior furnishings, transportation, toys, etc.
- Images: digitized, photographic, illustrated, etc.

Appendix C: Planning Your Unit of Study

Unit Overview

Unit Title: _____

Enduring Idea: (This needs to be *really* important—art and life issues that have lasting human importance and appear to be a continual concern to humans at different times and in different cultures.)

_____

_____

_____

Rationale: (Why is it important for students to understand the Enduring Idea?)

_____

_____

_____

Key Concepts about the Enduring Idea: (Note that these are important ideas—ASPECTS of the Enduring Idea.)

_____

_____

_____

Key Concepts about Art/Visual Culture: (Note that these are important ideas about art/visual culture, also related to the Enduring Idea, that will be addressed in the unit of study.)

_____

_____

_____

Essential Questions: (What questions will guide the investigation of the Enduring Idea and Key Concepts?)

_____

_____

_____

Unit Objectives: (Note that these are UNIT, not specific lesson, objectives. What "big" things will students understand as a result of investigations in this unit of study?)

_____

_____

_____

National, State, or Local Standards: (What standards will be targeted in this unit of study?)

_____

_____

_____

Assessment:

Evidence: (How will students DEMONSTRATE their understanding of the Enduring Idea and Key Concepts of the unit? What "end-of-unit" performance task(s) will they complete to demonstrate that they have met the UNIT objectives?)

_____

_____

_____

Levels and Criteria: (How will students and others know that they have completed the task successfully? What criteria will be used to judge partial, essential, or exemplary achievement?)

Exemplary:

_____

_____

_____

Essential:

_____

_____

_____

Partial:

_____

_____

_____

Overview of Lessons

Note that this is still an *overview,* not your detailed plan. When you describe the "action" in each lesson and indicate what students will learn from it, you are better able to see how the lessons relate to one another, are sequenced, and how they collectively build toward the unit objectives. The number of lessons in a unit will depend upon what is needed to develop targeted understandings.

In planning the lessons within the unit, make sure that you consider the following:

1   How will you help students connect the enduring idea/theme to the students' lives?

2   How will you build the students' knowledge base about the enduring idea/theme as it relates to life?

3   How will you build the students' knowledge base about the enduring idea/theme as it occurs in art (art criticism, art history, aesthetics)?

4   How will you engage students with exploring, questioning, and problematizing the enduring idea/theme through artmaking?

Lesson 1:
What will students do?

_____

_____

_____

What will students learn from this?

_____

_____

_____

Lesson 2:
What will students do?

_____

_____

_____

What will students learn from this?

_____

_____

_____

Lesson 3:
What will students do?

_____

_____

_____

What will students learn from this?

_____

_____

_____

Lesson 4:
What will students do?
What will students learn from this?

_____

_____

_____

Lesson 5:
What will students do?
What will students learn from this?

_____

_____

_____

Planning For Artmaking
(Use the format below for thinking about how you will engage students in meaningful artmaking.)

Artmaking Problem How will students explore/question the Enduring Idea/Topic? **Conceptual Strategy** What conceptual strategy will help students question, explore, or problematize the enduring idea? How can you help students develop new perspectives/viewpoints about the Enduring Idea/Topic?	**Personal Connections**
Artmaking Boundaries What limits will you place on students' artmaking? (media, subject matter, visual form, scale, techniques, context)	**Technical Knowledge**

Artworks, Artists, Artifacts

Select an optional number of artworks to assist you in developing a knowledge base and, ultimately, the targeted understandings of the Enduring Idea and Key Concepts. For each key artwork, artist and/or artifact, note why you are using it.

Key Artwork/artist/artifact:

_____
_____
_____

Reason for including:

_____
_____
_____

Key Artwork/artist/artifact:

_____
_____
_____

Reason for including:

_____
_____
_____

OTHERS (not KEY artworks, artists, or artifacts but ones that will be useful examples to help develop a knowledge base and understandings.)

_____
_____
_____

Significant Facts about Artworks, Artists, Artifacts

(Note that it is important that you are familiar with the artworks, artists, artifacts, and the contexts in which they have been created and used. Identifying this information should be part of the planning process.)

Artwork/artist/artifact:

_____
_____

Significant facts:

_____
_____

Artwork/artist/artifact:

_____
_____

Significant facts:

_____
_____

Detailed Instructional Plan

For each lesson in the unit, create a plan that will provide students opportunities to develop their knowledge base, learn and practice important skills, and apply new knowledge through disciplined inquiry.

LESSON NUMBER _____

Enduring Idea/Theme: (repeated here, each time, as a reminder)

_____

Key Concepts Addressed in this Lesson: (from the original list in overview)

_____
_____
_____

Lesson Summary: (a description of the lesson, noting how it relates to the enduring idea and how it builds upon previous lessons and prepares for lessons that follow)

_____
_____
_____

Lesson Objective(s): (Students will know, be able to, evidence, demonstrate, apply, etc. The number of objectives for a lesson will vary.)

1 Students will:

_____
_____

2 Students will:

_____
_____

3 Students will:

_____
_____

4 Students will:

_____
_____

Standards: (What national, state, or local standards are addressed in this lesson?)

_____
_____
_____

Required Knowledge, Skills, and Dispositions: (Consider what knowledge, skills, and dispositions will be important for students to have in order to meet lesson objectives. By articulating these, you are better able to design more effective instructional strategies/activities within the lesson.)

KNOWLEDGE:

_____
_____
_____

SKILLS:

_____

_____

_____

DISPOSITIONS:

_____

_____

_____

Assessment: (How will students and you know that they have learned what is intended? Note both formal and informal assessment strategies. Note also that instructional strategies can sometimes function as assessment strategies.)

Objective #1:

_____

_____

_____

Instructional Strategies/Activities: (How will you facilitate learning and sequence instruction so that students will be able to meet lesson objectives? The number of strategies/activities will vary.)

Objective #2:

_____

_____

_____

1 (engage)

_____

_____

Objective #3:

_____

_____

_____

2 (develop)

_____

_____

Objective #4:

_____

_____

_____

3 (develop)

_____

_____

4 (develop)

_____

_____

5 (close)

_____

_____

Appendix D: Sample Worksheets

Worksheet 1:

Building a Knowledge Base: Describing a Particular Place (My Place)

This worksheet may be used to build students' knowledge prior to artmaking about "place."

Display?	Aromas?	Lighting?	Sound?	Pathways?
Surfaces?	Corners?	Social Class?	Gender?	Social Interaction?
Prohibitions?	Permissions?	Architectural details?	Space?	Images?

Building a Knowledge Base about "Place" (based on your grid)

What makes this place a place?

What is most obvious about this place?

What is not obvious about this place?

How does this place affect human behavior?

How has human behavior affected this place?

How is this place about choice?

Worksheet 2:
Digging for Personal Stories
This worksheet may be used to help students develop ideas for creating narrative artworks.

Family Stories You know the kind . . . the ones that others tell about you, the ones that you tell about your siblings or parents or grandparents or that favorite aunt or uncle of yours.	**School Stories** Embarrassing moments, the day the biology lab flooded. . . . You remember, don't you?
Sports Stories The one that got away . . . your first touchdown or goal . . . the day you won the ribbon . . . training for the marathon . . . cycling the mountain until you got the flat tire . . .	**Friendship Stories** How you met . . . the best day ever . . . meeting . . . special times . . . sad times . . .
His/Her Stories Your ancestors and how they came to America; your family home and its history; your town, your city, your region, and their important stories. . . .	**Hero Stories** Special people and what they did . . . in history . . . in myth . . . in your lifetime . . . People you know up close . . . people you know from afar . . .

Worksheet 3:

Planning Performance Tasks

Use this worksheet as you plan for students to demonstrate understanding of the Enduring Ideas, Key Concepts, and the targeted knowledge and skills of the unit.

UNIT TITLE: _____

Enduring Idea:

_____

Key Concepts:

_____

_____

_____

Knowledge and Skills:

_____

_____

_____

• **Goal:** _____

• **Role:** _____

• **Audience:** _____

• **Situation:** _____

• **Production or Performance:** _____

• **Standards for Success:** _____

Index

visuality, 121–122, 128
Vogue magazine, 126, 127

W
Walker, John, 121
Walkup, Nancy, v
Wallace Smith Elementary School, 87
Warner, Charles, 70
Web quests, 79
Westat, v
"What Does a Friend Look Like? Friendship in Art" unit, 82
Whitehead, Alfred North, 23
Wiggins, Grant, 20
"Will Henry Stevens and a Place for Me" unit, 46, 48, 50
Wilson, Brent, 41
Wilson's list for art teachers, 41

Wood, Grant, 26, 112
Woodland High School, 12, 70, 81, 96
word wall, 79
worksheets, 74, 84, 98, 150–151
writing, 3–4, 16, 79, 84
Wulliger, Marilyn, v

Y
Yamane, Lynne, 14
Young Mother Sewing (Cassatt), 91
Youngs, Anne, 76, 77
Yrabedra, Ron, v

Z
Zellweger, Renee, 126–127